NORTHERN ROSE

The history of

WEST YORKSHIRE ROAD CAR CO. LTD.

Keith A. Jenkinson

An Autobus Review Publication

ISBN 0 907834 13 2

First published August 1987.

Typeset by x height phototypesetting, Headingley, Leeds.

Printed by Waddington & Sons Ltd., Todmorden.

Autobus Review Publications Ltd.,
42 Coniston Avenue, Queensbury,
Bradford BD13 2JD.

FOREWORD

It gives me very great pleasure to write the Foreword to a new history in the West Yorkshire Road Car Co. Ltd., which has been very ably produced by Keith Jenkinson, whose style and enthusiasm has always attracted so much interest from both the professional and enthusiast.

I look upon this book as a dedication to all those staff who have given loyal service to the company throughout the history of the last eighty one years.

The company now moves forward into a new era of privatisation and new ownership which has emerged from the 1985 Transport Act, which embraced deregulation and new competition.

I have been very proud to be Managing Director of the company for the last nine years and I am sure that it is now poised for continued success as I hand over to Giles Fearnley, the newly appointed Managing Director from 1 August 1987. I am confident that the future already mentioned is assured.

Brian M. K. Horner,
Managing Director,
West Yorkshire Road Car Co. Ltd.
July 1987.

ACKNOWLEDGEMENTS

Although a previous history of West Yorkshire Road Car Co. Ltd. and its predecessors was written several years ago, much new information has since come to light which it is hoped will justify this completely new volume which traces the developments and progress of this important operator up to its recent return to the private sector.

While much of the detail contained in this book has been drawn from my own personal records and memories, mention must be made of the many other people without whose help it would have been impossible to undertake the task of assembling so much information and so many photographs. In particular I am most grateful to Mr. Brian M. K. Horner, Managing Director of West Yorkshire Road Car Co. Ltd. who asked me to record the history of his company once again and who made available to me all the the surviving records and archive material relating to West Yorkshire and its predecessors. These provided a wealth of previously unknown detail, especially of the early years. My thanks are also extended to Mr. Tom Gedfrey for his help over many years and to Mr. J. C. W. Halliday and Mr. G. H. F. Atkins and many others for allowing me to use their excellent photographs to illustrate this volume. So many people have played their part towards the compilation of this work that it is impossible to name each individually, and I hope that they will each accept my sincere thanks for their assistance. In addition, I would place on record my gratitude to Mr. Giles Fearnley, the company's new Managing Director for bringing this history up to date and explaining the conclusion of the recent privatisation of West Yorkshire.

I hope that the following pages will evoke many memories and will provide much of interest to all those who read this history. To those wishing to keep up to date with future developments within West Yorkshire Road Car Co. Ltd., such information is regularly published in the monthly magazine 'Bus Fayre'.

Keith A. Jenkinson,
Queensbury,
Bradford,
August 1987.

ROAD CAR MAKES ITS DEBUT

Although the West Yorkshire Road Car Co. Ltd. has been in existence for sixty years, its foundations were laid during the early part of the century when its predecessor, Harrogate Road Car Co. Ltd., was formed to run a number of bus services within that town. Even before this however, Harrogate had been served by a number of small operators who ran horse-drawn vehicles from the town centre to the suburbs and names such as Bob Dent who provided a service to Bilton and New Park; W. Pyne of Starbeck who operated to his home district and the Harrogate Carriage Company who specialised in local excursions will long be remembered as pioneers of public transport in the area.

The railway had first reached Harrogate on 21 July 1848 when the Leeds and Thirsk Railway Company completed their line from Church Fenton into the town, terminating this at Brunswick Station, diagonally opposite the Brunswick Hotel near the present Trinity Church. On this same date, the horse bus service which had previously connected Harrogate with the former end of the railway line at Spofforth ceased, but then began to connect the new Harrogate station with other parts of the town. Soon afterwards, a further horse-bus service was commenced connecting Starbeck station with Harrogate and Knaresborough and although this continued for many years, the earlier service to Brunswick station ceased on 1 June 1852 after which various hotels began to provide horse-drawn transport to and from the railway terminal.

As the population of Harrogate increased (from 3,500 in 1851 to over 20,000 by 1897), this prompted an interest in various forms of internal transport within the town and on 25 May 1898 a proposal was made to build a tramway linking Harrogate to Knaresborough and a more local Harrogate circular line. This proposal met with a stormy reception from the Town Council however, as it was feared that if their spa resort was defaced by electric traction poles and clanking trams, this would drive away many of the visitors who came to Harrogate to enjoy the quiet and solitude of the town.

Not easily deterred however, those pioneers of electric tramways continued to make approaches to Harrogate for permission to introduce this then new form of transport and in June 1902 the British Electric Traction Company submitted plans for the Council's approval. This prompted Harrogate to look seriously – for the first time – at the possibility of allowing trams to operate within their town and, before agreeing to the B.E.T. proposal, they decided to investigate the running of trams themselves and formed a Tramway Committee for this purpose. After visiting several tramway systems in various parts of Britain, the Council agreed in July 1902 to seek powers to provide a tramway system, and two months later proposed three routes: Leadhall Lane to New Park; Station Square to Forest Lane Head and Dragon Road to Bilton. It was proposed that all three routes would be of single track with passing loops. Before the Harrogate proposals were submitted to Parliament however, thoughts were turned to alternative types of transport and on 30 September, a steam bus from Scarborough was demonstrated to the Council. Now in a dilemma, the Council was divided as to which type of transport system to select, and the discussions continued.

Meanwhile, by 1897 Mr. E. O. Hepper of the Crown Hotel Mews was operating a horse bus service from Oatlands to Starbeck and when the Harrogate Carriage Company was formed on 1 April 1898, Mr. Hepper, who became a director of this new company, transferred his service to them. At around this same time, Mr. Bob Dent was also operating a successful horse bus service from New Park and Bilton to Station Square using a two-horse double decker.

Following the steam bus demonstration to the Council in September 1902, a Mr. Norman MacDonald of Edinburgh applied to the Council for permission to provide a motor bus service in Harrogate but surprisingly in view of their own recent discussions, the Council refused this, adding 'that they did not at the present time see any need for motorbuses in the town'. The Council themselves obviously had not discounted the possibility of running their own transport system however, as enquiries continued to be made to this end and as late as February 1905 they were still gaining information from other operators in a bid to find the most efficient form of transport. Their attention was however turning more and more towards the motor bus rather than electric trams and the latter seemed doomed never to appear within the town.

Before any decisions were taken, Messrs. Berry & Snell, Auctioneers and Estate Agents in Harrogate who had since the previous year been advertising horse buses for hire, in November 1904 requested the Council to grant them a licence to operate motor buses from the town centre to outlying areas. Surprisingly in view of past decisions, they were informed that such licences would be granted subject to them being annually and the buses concerned being submitted for inspection and approval. Subsequently, on 19 May 1905 a 2-cylinder petrol driven Wolseley 16-seat bus was demonstrated in Harrogate by the local Wolseley agents, Johnson & Co. of 28 Montpellier Parade (the address of the Harrogate Road Car Co. booking office in later years). Although this was favourably reported (and the Harrogate Advertiser suggested that Johnson & Co. should be rewarded with the granting of a licence to operate a bus service in the town), the earliest delivery date given by Wolseley for a bus of that type was a year hence, and as a result, no order was placed.

Following four years of deliberations, Harrogate Council finally rejected a tramway system at their meeting on 15 September 1906, favouring instead a motor bus or electric bus service which it was felt would cause less congestion in the town centre streets. Realising that if they proceeded with plans to operate their own transport system it could take up to two years to gain the necessary powers, it was at last agreed that it may be better to authorise independent operators to run bus services within the town and as a result, on 26 November Mr. A. H. Marshall was granted a licence to commence a service from Oatlands to the town centre using a Chelmsford steam bus. This route was begun immediately and from the outset was a great success and welcomed by all the residents of that area of Harrogate.

Seeing the potential of this new service and the possibility of additional routes to other parts of the town, a local builder, Herbert Raworth, who was at that time concerned in the development of the Leeds Road area approached Mr. Marshall with a suggestion that they could together, and with other interested parties, form a new company and put the mechanically-propelled bus firmly into the Harrogate scene. The outcome of this approach was witnessed on 24 December 1906 when Raworth, Marshall and a number of other local businessmen registered a new company under the title of Harrogate Road Car Co. Ltd. Surprisingly, although it was his brainchild, of the eleven original shareholders, Herbert Raworth held the least shares (99 of the 4593 allotted), although at the first director's meeting he was elected temporary secretary and temporary manager of the newly formed company, Henry Norman Rae being elected chairman. The registered office was set up at 7, Station Bridge, Harrogate and operations began on 29 December 1906 with Marshall's Chelmsford steam bus working 21 daily departures from Station Square to Oatlands and return and 18 to Starbeck and return. No service was operated on Sundays. As a result of the popularity of this service, it was found necessary to obtain a second bus and this was duly ordered from Clarkson's of Chelmsford in early January, this (registered F1802) entering service on the first day of the following month.

Realising that one vehicle would not be sufficient to cater for the services it was proposed to operate, the new company immediately began to look for additional buses and were assisted by the fact that on 28 December 1906, the Torquay & District Motor Omnibus Co. Ltd. held a shareholders meeting at which the directors intimated that it was proposed to sell the company's eight Chelmsford steam buses due to the pending operation of trams in the town. This 'new' form of transport obviously worried the directors, who felt that they would be unable to compete if the trams ran through the main thoroughfares of the town and forced them to find new routes. Hearing of these difficulties, Harrogate Road Car Co. immediately entered into negotiations for the purchase of all eight of these steam buses and an agreement was ultimately signed at the Prince of Wales Hotel, Harrogate on 8 January 1907 for the purchase of these buses, plus two bus bodies for a sum of £2,400. It was agreed that the Torquay company would be allowed to continue to use them until Saturday 9 February, after which delivery must be made to Harrogate as quickly as possible. At first it was decided that the buses and two spare bodies should be sent to Harrogate via the Great Central Railway, although this was later changed to the Midland Railway Company who loaded the vehicles on 14 February, delivering them to their new owners a couple of days later.

Initially, the Harrogate company employed three drivers but upon receipt of eight additional vehicles, it was clear that more would be needed. The former manager of the Torquay company, a Mr. Fuller, accepted the position of garage manager of Harrogate Road Car Co. and upon his move from Torquay he brought with him five experienced drivers and two mechanics. Meanwhile, the company was engaged in a search for garage premises in Harrogate from which to operate their vehicles and in January 1907 took on lease the whole of the premises of Wardman & Sons in Myrtle Road.

Before delivery of the eight steam buses from Torquay was made, their former owners asked Harrogate Road Car if they would be prepared to resell some of these to a third party, but at a director's meeting on 11 February it was resolved to retain all eight in view of the new services which were planned. These services were to run from the town centre to Bilton and New Park; Harlow Moor Drive and Harlow Hill; Duchy Road and Knaresborough and in view of the steam buses needing frequent supplies of water, it was agreed that water mains be installed at Harlow Hill; Starbeck; Duchy Road and New Park during March.

On arrival in Harrogate, the eight former Torquay buses were immediately put to work alongside the one purchased new by the Road Car Co. and by 7 March all the new routes except that to Knaresborough were being operated. Such was the success of these that during April Saturday frequencies were increased on the routes to Duchy Road; Bilton/New Park; Starbeck and Oatlands routes. Immediately following this, on 27 April, the new Knaresborough service commenced, the fare being 3d each way.

Herbert Raworth was appointed Managing Director on 15 April 1907 and, in his new role he at once began to look for expansion in various fields. As early as 29 April he was offering the steam buses for hire for private parties during the hours in which they were not required for normal service and during the following month one was hired out to take a party from Harrogate to Ripley to an evening concert for 30/- while another was hired to the YMCA for a day excursion for £4. The company policy was however that no vehicles would be hired out on Sundays – a day on which their services did not run either. Seeing the possibility of further development in the private hire field,

The first Chelmsford steam bus to be bought by the new Company was delivered in January 1907 and is seen here at the New Park terminus of the service from Harrogate.

New in 1905 to the Torquay Motor Omnibus Co., this Chelmsford steam bus, T468 was purchased by Harrogate Road Car Co. in February 1907 along with all the other buses from this Devonshire operator. It is seen here on the Bilton/New Park service.

HARROGATE ROAD CAR COMPANY, LIMITED.

MOTOR OMNIBUS SERVICE.

COMMENCING SATURDAY, MARCH 2nd, 1907, and until further notice.

OATLANDS.

STATION SQUARE: .. 8-10 .. 8-35 .. 9-0 .. 9-30 a.m.
and every half-hour till 8-0 p.m.
Saturdays till 10 p.m. FARE 2d.

OATLANDS: ..... 8-25 .. 8-50 .. 9-15 .. 9-45 a.m.
and every half-hour till 8-15 p.m.
Saturdays till 10-15 p.m. FARE 2d.

DUCHY ROAD.

STATION SQUARE: .. 8-5 .. 8-30 .. 9-0 .. 9-30 a.m.
and every half-hour till 8-0 p.m.
Saturdays till 10-0 p.m. FARE 2d.

DUCHY ROAD: .... 8-20 .. 8-45 .. 9-15 .. 9-45 a.m.
and every half-hour till 8-15 p.m.
Saturdays till 10-15 p.m. FARE 2d.

BILTON and NEW PARK.

STATION SQUARE: 8-35 .. 9-0 .. 9-30 .. 10-0 a.m.
and every half-hour till 8-0 p.m.
Saturdays till 10-0 p.m. FARE 2d.

BILTON & NEW PARK:
8-20 .. 8-50 .. 9-15 .. 9-45 a.m.
and every half-hour till 8-15 p.m.
Saturdays till 10-15 p.m.

Between Station Square and Grange Avenue

STARBECK.

LEAVE STATION SQUARE: .. 8-45 .. 9-15 .. 9-45 a.m.
and every half-hour till 7-45 p.m.
Saturdays till 9-45 p.m. FARE 2D.

LEAVE STARBECK: ..... 9-0 .. 9-30 .. 10-0 a.m.
and every half-hour till 8-0 p.m.
Saturdays till 10-0 p.m. FARE 2D.

Between Station Square & Westmoreland Street, 1D.

HARLOW MOOR DRIVE.

LEAVE STATION SQUARE: 9-15 .. 10-15 .. 11-15 a.m.
and every hour till 7-15 p.m.
Saturdays till 9-15 p.m. FARE 2D.

LEAVE HARLOW MOOR DRIVE:
9-30 .. 10-30 .. 11-30 a.m.
and every hour till 7-30 p.m.
Saturdays till 9-30 p.m. FARE 2D.

HARLOW HILL.

LEAVE STATION SQUARE: 9-45 .. 10-45 .. 11-45 a.m.
and every hour till 7-45 p.m.
Saturdays till 9-45 p.m. FARE 2D.

LEAVE HARLOW HILL: . 10-0 .. 11-0 a.m.
and every hour till 8-0 p.m.
Saturdays till 10 p.m. FARE

This copy of the Harrogate Road Car Co. time table dated 2 March 1907 also shows the fares charged on each route at that time.

Mr. Fuller was instructed to design a new open body for fitting to one of the steamers and to have this built at the lowest tender.

During May 1907, the registered office of Road Car was transferred from 7 Station Bridge to Myrtle Road where the garage was situated, and at this same time an inspector was appointed for the duration of the summer. The drivers who, until this time had been wearing their own clothing for work were given the luxury of waterproof (oilskin) coats paid for by the company and this obviously made their lives a little more comfortable, especially during bad weather.

Seeking additional vehicles, Mr. Fuller was instructed in May to attend Habgoods sale and to purchase his steam motor carrier at not more than £40. This he successfully did and upon arrival at Myrtle Road, this was fitted with the new open body for use both in service and for private hire. Certain timetable alterations were made towards the end of June when the words 'weather permitting' were added to the Knaresborough service.

Although insurance to run two additional buses was taken out in July, it is not known whether the second of these was bought new or secondhand, the first obviously being the open-bodied vehicle purchased at the Habgood sale. By now, the Chelmsfords were becoming troublesome and several were suffering from badly-leaking boilers. As a result, it was decided to visit Lancaster to make enquiries regarding a new type of boiler recommended by Clarksons (the manufacturers of the Chelmsfords) and subsequently boilers of the new type were ordered.

Following numerous discussions, it was agreed to build a new garage for the growing fleet and to this end a site in Hookstone Road was examined on 11 September. This proved unsuitable however and after negotiations with Wardmans, the owners of the company's present garage, it was agreed to purchase this in October before the expiry of the existing lease. An additional garage and some land adjacent to the Myrtle Road premises was also purchased from Wardmans to enable enlargement of the premises when this was needed.

In September 1907, Mr. Fuller visited Windermere to examine a pair of steam buses offered for sale by the Lake District Road Traffic Co. Ltd. and later that month visited Wistaston to view two vehicles for sale by Samuel Jackson & Sons. It is understood that two of these were purchased (the exact two being unknown) and these were used towards the end of October to double the service on the Starbeck and Bilton routes.

Finally, in November the company allowed postmen in uniform to travel on any route except that to Knaresborough for a 1d any distance fare following representations from the Postmans Federation and at the same time reduced all their fares to the same level as was being charged by opposition operators.

Following a highly successful first year of operating bus services in and around Harrogate, the company began to look towards even further expansion and in January 1908 accepted an offer from a Mr. Mann to hire to them a motor bus for evaluation purposes. At this same time the Duchy Road service had to be temporarily suspended due to the bus which was used on this service having to be returned to Clarksons for repair. A further attempt made to encourage passengers away from their competitors, Road Car offered books of 13 1d tickets at a discount price of 1/-, which proves that the West Yorkshire PTE saverstrips of the 'eighties are not nearly as new as one has been led to believe!

The company's main competitor had been the General (Harrogate) Motor Car Co. which had been started by Mr. H. Thorpe during the latter part of 1907 with a route from Station Square to Oatlands. Mr. Thorpe was to have but a short life as a bus operator however, for in February 1908 he made an approach to Road Car, offering them his business and fleet. This was duly taken up and on 26 February his business and two buses were purchased. The buses concerned were both Chelmsfords which Thorpe had bought secondhand and both dated from 1905. At this time, two of Road Car's own buses were away at Clarksons for major repair and they thus welcomed the two new additions to their fleet so as to enable them to continue their services which all operated with a half-hourly frequency except the Starbeck and Bilton routes which were every quarter hour.

As well as experiencing good receipts from their services, the company had also expanded its private hire operations and placed orders for two further open bodies for fitting to Chelmsford chassis. Being the main operator of mechanically-propelled vehicles, they had taken much of their private hire and excursion trade from the Harrogate Carriage Co. who still retained a 100% horse-drawn fleet.

An Extraordinary General Meeting of shareholders was held on 5 May at which it was resolved to alter the Articles of Association to read 'No invitation to the public to subscribe for any shares or debentures of the company shall at any time be issued or made', thus altering the status of the company from public to private.

The winter timetable, introduced towards the end of September provided one bus for the Oatlands service, one for Bilton, two for Starbeck and one for Harlow Hill and Duchy Road with additional service on the Bilton route on Saturdays. The Knaresborough service was withdrawn for the winter due to lack of passengers, although it was to be re-introduced again for the following summer. Sunday running was still not allowed.

A fitting end to the year came when the Directors agreed on 16 December to permit employees to have collecting boxes in their buses for the Christmas period.

Following the developments of the previous two years, 1909 proved uneventful with services being maintained at their previous level and no new routes introduced. An extension was added to the garage at Myrtle Road and the fares on all services were altered with effect from 22 March when on the Starbeck route the fare from Stations Square to Westmoreland Street corner was fixed at 1d; from Station Sqaure to Granby Terrace was 1½d and the 1d section on the Oatlands route was abolished. Commencing on 5 October an additional vehicle was also operated on the Starbeck service on Saturdays when the service requirement was 6 vehicles (4 buses on weekdays). Although an offer was made by Stevens Ltd. to demonstrate a petrol-electric vehicle to the company, this was not taken up and the Chelmsfords continued to reign supreme, despite their operational problems.

Similarly, 1910 passed without any major changes and it was not until November that the company began to realise the need for new buses for use during the following summer. After first considering further steam vehicles, they turned their attention to the more modern petrol engine chassis which they believed would give them more versitility in their operaions. After some discussion, it was decided in November to purchase two Durham Churchill charabancs and one Durham Churchill chassis at a total cost of around £1,000 and these were duly ordered in the following January. Soon after these arrived – in time for the summer season – the question of overcrowding on the Bilton route was raised which had caused damage to the axles and springs of the buses concerned. Mr. Fuller reported on a pair of Clarkson double deckers he had seen and on a vehicle he had been informed of which was for sale in York. Following instructions to investigate further, the two double deckers were duly purchased whilst negotiations were entered into regarding the hire of the Commer charabanc at York for a trial period after which, if considered suitable, it would be purchased. As a consequence of the arrival of these additional vehicles, the old bus bodies removed from the Chelmsfords converted to charabancs were sold.

To accommodate the growing fleet, additional garage accommodation was now urgently needed and a further property was purchased in Myrtle Road in June 1912 for this purpose. Meanwhile, consideration was being given to the acquisition of one or two new charabancs and although this was left in abeyance, the need became more urgent following the introduction of a new charabanc service to Knaresborough by the North Eastern Railway Co. during the summer months. This led the company to order two new 'torpedo' bodies for Durham Churchills C1695 and C4494, although these did not materialise until early in 1913, and a new Commer which arrived in July 1912. Rather than increase the fleet during 1912, it remained static, for on the arrival of the new Commer, the small Chelmsford – C1711 – which had been acquired from Thorpe in 1908 was scrapped and its body sold. Until this time, the buses had all carried a green livery (the charabancs being cream), but on 14 October 1912 it was agreed that one of the double deckers should be repainted Heliotrope. Following numerous complaints by passengers of the condition of the fleet at that time, a hasty repainting programme was put underway in November and by the end of the year all were sporting the new colour.

The Chelmsfords were by now way past their best and were causing increasing problems in service as well as attracting unwelcome police attention. One prosecution had already been made in respect of the emission of steam on a public highway, and fearing others might follow, the company decided in January 1914 to order three new Daimler 27-seat single deckers for use on town services. These arrived in April and replaced the steamers on the 15th of that month on the Oatlands, Starbeck and Bilton/New Park routes. No sooner had they settled in on their new duties however than they were impressed by the War Office who were at that time requisitioning large numbers of petrol-engined vehicles for use by the Army in the new war. Having had their bodies removed at Myrtle Road, the chassis left Harrogate on 20 September to form the basis of Military lorries. Fortunately, the Chelmsfords which they had replaced earlier in the year had not yet been sold and these had to be hurriedly returned to service to take up the Daimlers duties.

Believing that the same fate may befall any further petrol-engined buses they may purchase, the company decided to wait a while before placing any further orders. Eventually, in September 1915 after examining the specification of new Caledon and McCurd chassis, the Directors decided to visit Morecambe where some McCurds were running and, if they found these to be satisfactory, would order this make for their own fleet. Following this visit across the Pennines, one complete McCurd single decker was ordered (with detachable windows and storm curtains) in September 1915 together with three McCurd chassis which were to be fitted with the almost new bodies removed from the Daimlers. Soon after these were delivered, a further two complete McCurd buses were ordered as was an additional chassis (January 1916) and at this same time it was agreed to sell three of the old Chelmsford steam buses and the Chelmsford charabanc. The other important development of

Chelmsford steam bus C5919 was one of the vehicles acquired secondhand by Harrogate Road Car in 1907. In this view at Starbeck terminus it can be seen taking water from a specially installed main.

1915 was the fitting of electric lighting to the garage and office in August.

Soon after the new McCurds had arrived and had settled down in service, petrol shortages became acute and other methods of operation had to be quickly considered. Other than restore the ailing steamers to service yet again, gas propulsion seemed the only alternative and in 1917 the McCurds were all fitted with huge gas bags carried on their roofs and were converted to operate on this new form of energy. Agreement was reached with the Harrogate Gas Company for the supply of town gas from specially-equipped street lamps fitted with meters at Station Parade (near the railway station); Queen Victoria's Jubilee Monument in Victoria Avenue, and at Starbeck and New Park. In addition, the McCurd's were fitted with a one gallon petrol tank on their dash to enable them to continue to the next filling up point should they run out of gas unexpectedly.

With these large gas-filled bags on their roof, these vehicles were extremely difficult to drive in windy conditions, and one was indeed blown over into a field at the top of New Park Hill on one such occasion. The gas bags caused considerable speculation among the public, some of whom thought these carried water in case of air raids whilst others thought they were to offer protection if the bus itself was bombed. When they were being refilled with gas, rain which had collected in pools in the deflated fabric had a tendancy to give the embarking or waiting passengers an undesired shower whilst in high winds the fabric was sometimes torn, allowing the gas to escape and, on the occasions when the driver had forgotton to fill up his one gallon petrol tank, leaving the bus stranded in often inconvenient places.

whilst the Karriers were 28-seat charabancs, as were five Daimlers which were also purchased new at this same time.

Following the commencement by Brown of their service from Harrogate to Knaresborough on 29 September 1919, Road Car began to look for premises in the latter town at which they could establish a garage. This did not materialise however and the company continued to operate solely from their bases at Myrtle Road and the White Hart Hotel throughout 1920. No further additions were made to the fleet during this year and it was not until January 1921 that authorisation was given to purchase any new vehicles. On this occasion, the order called for three Karrier chassis with charabanc bodywork as replacements for the Durham Churchills which were to be sold upon the arrival of the new vehicles. A Lancia charabanc was also purchased during the year.

Competition again increased in 1922 when Harrogate Carriage Co. applied to run a service to Knaresborough on Wednesdays (market day) – although this did not actually begin until 1923 – and Charles & Oliver Holdsworth founded the Bilton Motor Co. and began a service from Bilton to Harrogate town centre. Jos. Robinson also reached the town with a service from Otley as did United Automobile Services with their service from Ripon. In an attempt to counter the challenge by Bilton Motor Co., Road Car began to offer books of coupon tickets in July with 14 2d tickets for 2/- and added further new vehicles to their fleet in the form of a pair of Karrier 30-seat single deck buses; a McCurd 26-seat bus and four Fiat 14-seat charabancs. These all carried the company's attractive Heather Violet livery and were distinctive against the yellow & black of Bilton Motor Co. and biscuit of the Carriage Company. Also ordered in July 1922 were two new bus

C3471, one of the McCurd single deckers is seen here during 1917 whilst being operated on town gas on the Oatlands Mount service in Harrogate. The inflated gas bag can be clearly seen on the roof with its temporarily-boarded retaining frame.

Toward the end of 1917, upon hearing that the White Hart Hotel stables and garage at that time occupied by Harrogate Carriage Co. were soon to be re-let, Road Car investigated the possibility of gaining a 10-year lease on these premises. These were required to house the private hire fleet which operated from a stand in Low Harrogate and it was thought they would also provide facilities for the taxi cabs under consideration at that time. Although the idea of running taxis was not proceeded with, the lease for the White Hart property was negotiated and signed in December. Harrogate Carriage Co. who were now operating a fleet of petrol-engined charabancs and taxi cabs, having sold all their remaining horse-drawn vehicles and horses on 16 October 1917, contacted Road Car in January 1918 with a view to an amalgamation of their respective businesses. Road Car, after giving consideration to this matter, did not feel that this was desirable at that time and so the two companies continued to compete.

The war ended and Harrogate Road Car now found themselves in an area of growing competition. The Carriage Co. was offering a wide range of excursions from Low Harrogate and B. Brown & Sons of Knaresborough were proposing to offer a new service between the two towns. To counter this, the company placed orders in January 1919 for 2 McCurd and 6 Karrier chassis with bodies to be decided upon later and all these arrived during the summer. The McCurds had 27-seat bus bodies

bodies for fitting to chassis already owned by the company, these being two of the vehicles delivered new in 1919.

Bilton Motor Co. suffered a major set back on 17 September 1922 when their depot caught fire, destroying both their Leyland buses plus two charabancs, a Rover car and three motor cycles which were in at the time. This caused them to temporarily abandon their service until 20 October when two replacement buses of the same make and type were delivered. Further competition entered Harrogate during 1923 when Warburton & Partridge began a service from Leeds; G. R. Smithson ran into the town from Spofforth; A.T.A. Transport Ltd. started a service to Pateley Bridge and Chapman & Jones also began to operate between these two towns. In addition, the Harrogate Carriage Co. had now entered the stage carriage field with services to Otley, Pateley Bridge and Knaresborough and were considering a further service to Wetherby and Boston Spa. Due to the increasing congestion around the railway station, in April 1923 all the bus departure points were moved away from Station Square to points along Raglan Street, Victoria Avenue and Station Parade, the Duchy Road serice being the odd one out starting at a new terminal point in Princess Sqaure.

Now being regarded as an important operator in the Harrogate area, Road Car were approached by Tillings of London in October 1923 asking them to consider an amalgamation which would increase their capital and allow

One of the McCurd single deckers with unusual open rear platforms is seen here operating the Bilton/ New Park Harrogate town service in the early 'twenties.

Above: One of Road Car's bus bodied Karriers operating on the Harrogate – Ilkley service.

Above right: WT2475, one of the Daimler buses showing the Harrogate Road Car Co. fleet name in equal-sized lettering works a Harrogate local service in 1924.

Right: This early post-world war I view shows one of the 1922 Karrier buses of Road Car on the Harrogate town service from Station Parade to Oatlands Mount.

WR9057, one of the Karrier K3 28-seat charabancs bought in 1921, stands at Low Harrogate with the Road Car Co. booking office in the background.

One of the pair of Leyland G6-type single deckers bought by Bilton Motor Co. in October 1922 to replace similar vehicles destroyed in their depot fire a month earlier is seen here with its driver and conductor.

further expansion. At this same time an approach was made by Harrogate Corporation who were considering running their own buses and saw Road Car as a solid foundation on which to build their own bus undertaking. Following discussions, the company (in November 1923) offered to sell the whole business, vehicles and property to the Corporation, but after realising the cost and commitment this would require, the Corporation decided not to proceed with their powers to become bus operators in their own right. Meanwhile, United Automobile Services had also made an approach, suggesting an amalgamation of their two companies, but this was not favoured by the Road Car board. This left Tillings as the only real contenders and at a meeting in London on the final day of the year with Tilling's directors, a formal agreement was reached which was presented to Road Car's shareholders at a special meeting on 7 January 1924. The agreement was 'that shareholders of Harrogate Road Car Co. Ltd. shall dispose of 75% of their shares to Thomas Tilling Ltd. at a price of £2 for each £1 share and that 75% shall be a minimum'. It went on to state that Tilling would purchase additional shares at similar prices, and that the transfer of shares shall be effective as soon as may be after the balance sheet for the year ended 31 December 1923 has been audited. The deal was eventually formalised on 26 March 1924 when Thomas Tilling Ltd. and the British Automobile Traction Co. Ltd. (a subsidiary of British Electric Traction Co. Ltd.) gained their controlling interest.

Prior to this taking place, Harrogate Road Car had on 1 February 1924 purchased the whole assets of Bilton Motor Co. including their property consisting of two houses and a garage in Mornington Terrace. Their three Leyland single deck buses and a Leyland charabanc were immediately transferred to their new owner's fleet although they continued to work from their old garage.

THE TILLING ERA ... & DISTRICT IS ADDED

Discussions regarding the inauguration of new services took place on 18 February when, although it was agreed that Sunday operations would still not be undertaken, weekday services should be arranged as soon as possible to serve outlying districts. Already the new Tilling influence was beginning to show and at this same meeting an order was placed for four new Tilling Stevens petrol-electric buses with solid rubber tyres and Tilling bodywork for delivery as soon as possible. The first of these new rear-entrance 36-seaters arrived on 26 June, the second following a day later and in their heather violet and white livery, both entered service immediately. The other two came on 7 and 11 July and bore the same livery. Once again needing additional garage space, further property was purchased in Myrtle Square during May to allow extensions to be made to the present garage. Furthermore, the lease was taken on an office at 28 Montpellier Parade, Harrogate which was located close to Road Car's excursion stand in Low Harrogate.

The new service develoment immediately ran into trouble when, in April, Ripon Council refused to grant licences for Road Car's proposed service to Harrogate and the company immediately lodged an appeal with the Ministry of Transport in an attempt to get this decision reversed. This it eventually did, but it took several months before the licences were actually granted for this service.

Still seeking to consolidate their position in Harrogate even further, the company opened negotiations in July with Harrogate Carriage Co. with a view to gaining a controlling interest in this old established business. The discussions were somewhat protracted and it was not until September that the directors were able to report that acceptances had been made to their offer. Thus, on 24 September 1924 the Carriage Co. became a subsidiary of Road Car, although it continued to be run as a separate entity and retained its individual livery of brown and biscuit, this having in 1913 replaced the original Carriage Co. colour of Royal blue and yellow which was applied to their first Thornycroft charabanc in 1911. Harrogate Carriage Co. was itself older than Road Car, having been registered on 23 May 1898 and at the time it passed to Road Car control, it operated a fleet of 14 buses and charabancs comprising two AEC 26-seat buses; a trio of Plaxton-bodied Thornycroft charabancs, a

The Fiat charabanc became popular with both West Yorkshire and Harrogate Carriage Co. during the early 'twenties. This West Yorkshire example carried Roe 16-seat bodywork.

One of Harrogate & District's Karrier 30-seat buses is pictured here whilst operating on the Harrogate to Pateley Bridge service in 1926.

Widdison-bodied Thornycroft charabanc; four Massey-bodied Fiat 14-seat charas; three Massey-bodied 18-seat Fiat buses and a Garford 18-seat charabanc. The services operated were from Harrogate to Knaresboroguh via Pannal and Follifoot; to Summerbridge (Saturdays only); Otley; Fountains Abbey; Wetherby & Tadcaster and to Pateley Bridge where the company maintained a tiny garage leased from Longster Bros.

Before gaining control of the Carriage Co., Road Car had in July 1924 received correspondence from Mr. Peel, proprietor of The Cream Bus Service Ltd. of Burley in Wharfedale in which he offered his fleet and Otley to Ilkley service to them. An offer was made in this respect but was not accepted by Mr. Peel, although this gentleman again offered his company in March 1925 for a sum of £3,000. On this occasion it was Road Car who declined and ultimately the Cream Bus Service was sold to S. Ledgard of Armley, Leeds.

A further four Tilling Stevens petrol-electric single deckers were ordered in September 1924 and it was agreed that if it was found possible to commence operations on the proposed Harrogate to Leeds service, a further four would be ordered. At this same meeting on 23 September it was resolved that the paintwork on the newly-ordered buses should be exactly similar in colour to that adopted by East Kent Road Car Co. and that this colour should be used on all future repaints of the existing fleet. Thus the red and white livery was born – a livery which in modified form still exists today on the company's fleet. It was however resolved at a meeting two months later that the new colours would not apply to the company's motor coaches which at that time were brown.

The new Leeds service eventually began at the start of November and as a consequence a further four Tilling Stevens petrol-electric single deckers were immediately ordered before the previous four had been received (these came between November '24 and January '25). Now that the company was running several services outside the Harrogate area, it seemed logical to alter the company's name to Harrogate and District Road Car Co. Ltd. as an indication of its wider operational sphere. Sanction of the shareholders to this effect was sought on 22 November and the 'new' name was formally adopted on 22 December 1924.

1925 began with a territorial agreement being signed with United Automobile Services on 15 January and was followed by the delivery of six, not four, new Tilling Stevens petrol-electrics in March and April. Further property was purchased at the

Tilling Stevens petrol-electric TS6 no.8 was one of the first batch to wear the company's new red & white livery. Seen here when new in December 1924 it proudly displays its Harrogate & District fleet name. As can be seen, no destination indicator was fitted at the front, the route being shown on slip boards below the side windows.

WU8512, a 1926 Tilling Stevens B9A with 31-seat Tilling rear entrance bodywork took fleet number 56 in the Harrogate District fleet. When delivered, it carried a route number stencil holder on its front roof dome, this being replaced by a bible destination board holder in 1930.

One of the Tilling-bodied Bean 14-seat buses delivered new to Harrogate & District in 1926 was used on the Wetherby-York route as pictured here.

corner of Myrtle Road and East Parade where it was agreed to immediately erect a new two-storey building at the rear of the houses (Sandal Villas) which at that time was used for stables. The new building was to be used as offices to allow the existing office accommodation alongside the garage to be modified to provide accommodation for the growing fleet.

Although the talks started with Blythe & Berwick of Bradford regarding the purchase of their omnibus operations collapsed during May, these were resurrected at a later date as will be seen in due course.

The Carriage Co. subsidiary was at this time making progress in its own right and in early May had purchased the local business of Wilsons Motors who had for some time been running in competition on the Wetherby/Boston Spa service and had been considering a new service to Knaresborough. Three vehicles were acquired with the Wilson business – a pair of Chevrolet 16-seat buses and a Reo 14-seat charabanc. To strengthen the fleet, Carriage Co. had bought a secondhand AEC chassis a month earlier and had temporarily fitted it with a spare charabanc body they already owned. This was replaced in October with a new bus body, making it much more useful for operation on stage carriage duties. By this time the three Massey-bodied 18-seat Fiat buses were causing many problems, frequently breaking down due to their heavy bodywork and a request was made to the parent company for urgent replacements. In answer, Harrogate & District transferred two of the ex.Bilton Motor Co. Leylands to the Carriage Co. at the start of August, although the Fiats were retained for occasional use when necessary. A new service was authorised from Harrogate to York in July 1925 – although this did not commence until the early spring in 1926, and as a result of poor loadings, the Wetherby/Boston Spa service was reduced from daily operations to Mondays, Wednesdays and Saturdays only with effect from mid-September. After this cut-back, it was worked by the ex.Wilson Chevrolets operating from the former company's dormy depot at Boston Spa.

Back at Harrogate & District, another six Tilling Stevens petrol-electrics were ordered in July with a request that these were to be fitted with higher-powered engines and a further six buses of this same type were ordered in September. Delivery of the first batch commenced in November and was completed during the following month whilst the second batch arrived between March and June 1926. Two Rudge Whitworth motor cycles were also ordered in September for the use of inspectors and an order was placed with Massey Bros. of Wigan for a saloon bus body to replace the old body of Daimler WT2475 which had become unfit for futher use.

Although the new arrivals increased the fleet size somewhat, in December one of the McCurds (C3482) was dismantled for spares and the body of the ex.Bilton Motor Co. Leyland RAF-type bus was sold, the chassis then being converted into a lorry for the company's own use.

Mr. Fuller, who had been the company's engineer since 1907 resigned at the end of October and was replaced by Mr. S. Kennedy from London.

As a company grew, so too did the need for additional vehicles for the senior staff and road inspectors and in January 1926 authority was given for the purchase of six small, light cars. Additionally it was agreed that an enclosed car for the use of management could be purchased should this be necessary at a later date. This was duly ordered in March in the form of a Bean car and at this same time an order was placed for 5 Bean omnibuses with 14-seat bodywork by Tilling. The latter began to arrive at the end of March and delivery was completed during the first week of June whilst the Bean car, a 4-door saloon finished in Royal blue also came in June. This was allocated to Mr. Kennedy, the company's chief engineer until his departure on 15 November 1926 to become chief engineer of Thomas Tilling Ltd., London and then passed to his successor, Mr. E. A. Barnwell.

Seeking additional operating bases as well as inaugurating new services, the company purchased an area of 939 sq.yds. of land in Roseville Road, Leeds in June upon which it was their intention to build a new bus garage. At the same time some property at Fisher Street, Knaresborough was bought for use as a bus stand and work was immediately put in hand to clear the site for this purpose.

Expansion was the uppermost thought in the company's mind at that time and negotiations were started with T. E. Sugden at the end of May for the purchase of Premier Transport (Keighley) Ltd., an important operator in the Keighley area with its own fleet of buses and owning two subsidiary companies – Nelson Haulage & Charabanc Co. Ltd. and the Silsden Haulage & Charabanc Co. Ltd. Reaching a conclusion, Premier and its subsidiaries were acquired on 14 July but, in similar fashion to Harrogate Carriage Co. Ltd., Premier was retained as a separate entity after absorbing its two subsidiaries. In addition to this giving Harrogate & District a strong foothold in Keighley and its surrounds with services from Keighley to Bingley; Oakworth; Laycock; Silsden and Thwaites Brow and a service from Shipley

Bearing the Silsden Haulage Chara Co. name, this Premier Transport subsidiary's 1915 Daimler was built for the London General Omnibus Co. but was delivered direct to the War Department. It passed to Harrogate & District control in 1926 and was withdrawn a year later. (The late R. Jackson)

to Bingley, it also added 16 more buses to the overall fleet, these being a mixed bag of Durham Chuchills, Daimlers, Karriers, SPAs and a former LGOC B-type single decker. Premier's livery of English Rose and cream was not dissimilar to that of Harrogate & District and this was retained.

Some two weeks before the Premier deal was completed, on 30 June the company took over a smaller, yet equally important operator at Tadcaster. This was Dibb & Warnes who traded under the title Leeds, Tadcaster & York Motor Service and used a green and white livery. Operating three routes – Leeds to York; Tadcaster to Wetherby and Bramham to Bramham Cross Roads they had a fleet of eight single deck buses, all of which were immediately transferred to their new owner.

Unlike many operators, Harrogate & District had continued to operate throughout the General Strike of 1926 and on 18 May received a letter from the Mayor of Harrogate congratulating them and thanking the staff for their continued service during this difficult period. Orders were placed in July for three Tilling Stevens Express-type single deckers (the B9) with Tilling bodywork and a further 12 of this same type were requested in September as replacements for the remaining old McCurds and a couple of other vehicles. Delivery of the first five of the B9s was made in September with the remaining ten arriving during the first couple of months of 1927. For the Premier fleet a total of 18 Tilling B9s and a trio of Bean 14-seaters were ordered and these too made their debut between the autumn of 1926 and spring of the following year. In addition to their new vehicles which replaced the motley collection acquired with the Premier business, the company took over the business of Alfred Longbottom of Thornton together with his Bradford – Denholme service in October.

Always in the market to extend their empire even further, the company made a successful offer for the business and fleet of J. J. Burns of Clifford near Boston Spa, gaining control on 28 March. Burns had a fleet of nine buses, all of which wore their owner's grey & black livery and operated two services from York to Bramham and from Leeds to Boston Spa via Bramham Cross Roads. The six Guys, a Ford model T, a Chevrolet and an Albion were all retained by their new owner as was Burns' garage at Boston Spa. The Ford T did not survive long in the main fleet however, being transferred to Premier after conversion to a lorry in July.

Following on the heels of the Burns acquisition came that of A. Warburton of Leeds who had a service from Leeds to Pool as well as the Leeds to Harrogate service which had run in competition with the Harrogate company since 1924. The Warburton fleet which consisted of four AECs and four ADCs was extremely modern, the oldest member being a mere twelve months old and these were regarded as a valuable asset by their new owner.

The third independent to fall victim of the ever-expanding Harrogate & District was H. Riley of Wetherby whose business and assets were acquired in November. With a fleet of seven buses of which four were modern Leyland PLSC Lions, Riley provided the company with a lucrative service from Leeds to Harrogate via Wetherby and a leased garage in the latter town.

Orders placed during 1927 for new buses called for no fewer than 31 Tilling Stevens B10A-type buses and 6 Tilling Stevens B10B-type charabancs in additon to a further Bean staff car and Morris Cowley car and of these, the first six of the B10s arrived during June. The year was not all a bed of roses however, for on 13 August disaster struck when one of the petrol-electric Tilling TS6s – WT8457 – was burnt out at Starbeck whilst in service.

Left: Pictured in Silsden in 1927 is West Yorkshire's subsidiary, Premier's WU8506, an all-Tilling B9A new in 1926. Note the route number stencil on the front roof dome. (The late R. Jackson)

Below: UM8861, one of Warburton's ADC 416A 32-seat Taylor-bodied buses on their Leeds – Harrogate service a few weeks before being taken over by West Yorkshire in July 1927.

Harrogate & District's other subsidiary, Harrogate Carriage Co., also had quite an eventful year in 1926. Requiring a new bus in June the manager produced details of an AEC he wished to purchase, but this was blocked by the parent company who felt that a Tilling Stevens B9 would be more suitable in view of their own orders for this type. As a result, a B9A was ordered and eventually arrived in September resplendent in full Carriage Co. livery. Such was its success alongside the other vehicles in the fleet that a further 4 were ordered in September for delivery in February 1927. The two ex.Wilsons Chevrolets 14-seaters were 'sold' to the parent company during July, thus reducing the fleet by one and, in order to gain even further rationalisation, all Carriage Co's clerical work was transferred from their office at 33 Montpellier Parade to Harrogate & District's offices at Myrtle Road at the end of November.

At the start of 1927 Mr. J. F. Heaton took over as Chairman of the company from H. G. Pilley who had held that office since 1909 and was one of the founder shareholders of the company. Soon after this change at the helm, it was agreed to build a new bus garage in Harrogate on land purchased at Grove Park Terrace whilst at Leeds where additional land had been acquired in Roseville Road during 1926, work on the construction of the new garage was progressing. Ilkley was the next area for development and in May land was bought in Hawkesworth Street to enable a new garage to be built, thus expanding the company's activities even further. Before leaving the subject of property it should be mentioned that in July a house in Tewit Well Road Harrogate was also purchased.

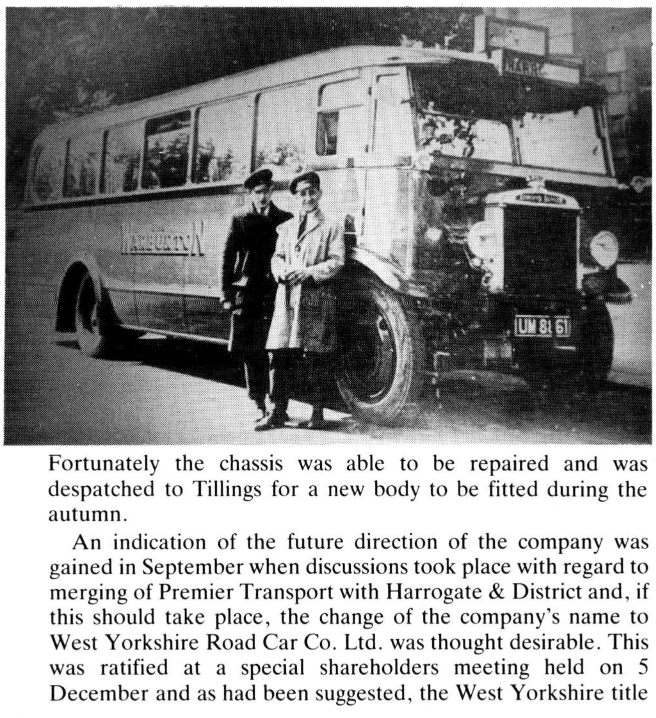

Fortunately the chassis was able to be repaired and was despatched to Tillings for a new body to be fitted during the autumn.

An indication of the future direction of the company was gained in September when discussions took place with regard to merging of Premier Transport with Harrogate & District and, if this should take place, the change of the company's name to West Yorkshire Road Car Co. Ltd. was thought desirable. This was ratified at a special shareholders meeting held on 5 December and as had been suggested, the West Yorkshire title

Amongst the first motor buses to be operated by Harrogate Road Car Co. was Commer BM983 with open sided, closed top charabanc bodywork. Seen here in Scarborough circa 1912, this chara incredibly survived until 1927 before its final withdrawal from service.

was adopted with immediate effect. Premier Transport was wound up on the final day of the year and its assets, vehicles and services were transferred to the new West Yorkshire company on 1 January 1928. From this same date it was agreed to lease the whole of the vehicles of Harrogate Carriage Co. Ltd. although these would retain their own distinctive livery and fleet name etc.

Prior to the demise of Premier, the Keighley company had in October purchased the goodwill and Skipton to Crosshills service of Skiptonian Motor Service, although no vehicles had changed ownership on this occasion. Furthermore, Harrogate & District had in November bought some land at Keighley adjoining Premier's garage in Anvil Street from Pickersgill Bros. to allow their premises to be extended and had bought further land at Roseville Road, Leeds for a similar purpose. Learning that a new company was to be formed under the name of Omnibus Stations Ltd. to acquire a site in Manchester to be used as a bus stand, Harrogate & District immediately applied for 2,500 shares in this company, despite at that time having no operations into that city.

EXPANSION TO WEST YORKSHIRE

West Yorkshire Road Car Co. Ltd. was now born and following the absorbtion of Premier their sights were set on further consolidation. This came on 16 January 1928 when the omnibus and charabanc part of the business of Blythe & Berwick of Bradford was purchased. The assets of this company included 41 omnibuses; 12 charabancs and 2 Ford lorries; seven lucrative services, freehold property at Edderthorpe Street and Thorncliffe Road, Bradford and at Cross Green, Otley and leasehold property at Otley Road, Shipley with buildings thereon. In additon the lease of premises at Chester Street, Bradford was also taken over and an undelivered order for 20 new Leyland PLSC Lion buses was to be honoured by the new owners.

Five Tilling Stevens B9As headed by former Premier 67 await their passengers during the Keighley holiday week of 1928. Note the short-lived roller destination indicators which were not long afterwards replaced by 'bible' destination boards and holders.

Quickly following this massive acquisition, at a meeting held on 11 February it was resolved that West Yorkshire Road Car Co. Ltd. should be converted into a public company, this being ratified on 29 March when it was agreed that 100,000 6½% cumlative preference shares of £1 each be issued on 12 April. These were quicly taken up by a number of subscribers including the B.E.T. who obtained 25,000 shares, the Argentine Great Western Railway Co. Ltd. with 10,000 and New York & General Trust Ltd. with 4,000 shares. Prior to this, the company had purchased new premises in Hammerton Street, Bradford from the liquidators of Cole, Marchant Thornley Ltd. and had made an agreement with Blythe & Berwick (who had retained their haulage business) to dispose of all plant and scrap metal contained in these buildings to allow their early conversion into a new bus garage. Meanwhile, work on the new Ilkley garage was nearing completion and opened in June.

The next operator to fall to the might of West Yorkshire was the Kildwick Motor Co. who had two Morris 14-seat buses and operated a service from Windhill to Shipley. This operator passed to the company on 26 May to be followed on 10 June by Keighley Bros. of Keighley. Although their services from Ilkley to Keighley, Keighley to Bradford Express and Skipton to York via Ilkley and Wetherby and 16 Leyland buses passed to West Yorkshire, it was decided to run the business on lines similar to those adopted in the case of Harrogate Carriage Co. and on 5 July Keighley Bros. (Omnibuses) Ltd. was registered, their 16 buses being transferred to the new company.

The dust had hardly settled when on 9 July the 3 Overland 14-seat buses and York – Strensall route of Strensall Ideal Motors was bought from its owner, Mr. A. Foy. This gave West Yorkshire even further strength in York and provided them with their first local service within the city. Two months later, on 8 September the last acquisition of 1928 was made when the 9-bus fleet of John Cole & Sons of Leeds was purchased. This brought the company a further three services – Leeds to Otley via

Resting outside Roseville Road depot at Leeds is former J. Cole & Sons' Strachan & Brown-bodied Albion PM28 136. The date of this photograph is believed to be around 1932.

Although ordered by Blythe & Berwick, Leyland Lion PLSC3 340 was not delivered until after that company had been taken over by West Yorkshire. Seen here ascending Cowpasture Road, Ilkley on the occasional summer service to the top of Ilkley Moor in 1932, its destination board was obviously a 'home-made' job. (The late R. Jackson)

Bramhope; Leeds to Ilkley via Otley and Leeds to Rawdon via West Park. All three services were operated jointly with G. F. Tate of Leeds and S. Ledgard of Armley and West Yorkshire now became their new partner.

On the vehicle front, a BSA motor cycle and 6 Leyland PLSC Lions were ordered during the year, these being in addition to the order for 20 taken over from Blythe & Berwick, 20 new Tilling Stevens B10A2s were specified and, more surprisingly, in May the company ordered its first double deck buses since the secondhand Chelmsford steamers acquired in 1911. The order placed called for 6 lowbridge Leyland TD1s with open staircase Leyland bodywork required for operation on the Bradford – Keighley route taken over from Blythe & Berwick. A further 4 buses of this type were ordered in September and another 10 were called for in November, bringing the total to 20. The first two of these arrived on 16 August and entered service immediately and a further four followed on 6 September. All six were operated from the new Hammerton Street, Bradford garage. To compensate for the numerous new additions to the fleet, a total of 36 obsolete single deckers of a variety of makes were withdrawn and sold.

During the past few years Harrogate Carriage Co. had continued to be operated as a separate subsidiary and, after vacating their garage at the Lancaster Hotel during February 1928 had moved into new accommodation at Myrtle Road. Two of the old Thornycroft charabancs had been fitted to run on pneumatic instead of solid tyres during the first month of 1927 whilst later in the year several of the older members of the fleet were sold and 2 new Tilling Stevens B10B all-weather charabancs were ordered.

Two more Tilling Stevens arrived in 1928 in the form of B10A2 buses and the fleet underwent a further reduction with the sale of 6 charabancs towards the end of that year. The short fall in vehicle numbers was made by the temporary loan of buses and charabancs from the West Yorkshire fleet, as and when these were required.

During May, a letter was received from Ribble Motor Services suggesting that the two companies should join together for the operation of services from Bradford to Morecambe and from Bradford to the Lake District. West Yorkshire gave this idea a warm reception and agreed that the Morecambe route should be started at the earliest possible date. On the opposite coast at Scarborough, an agreement was entered into with East Yorkshire Motor Services for part of the garage leased to them by Robinsons' Motors Ltd. to be used to house West Yorkshire vehicles, this commencing in September. Less happy was the refusal in August by Haworth U.D.C. to grant a licence for a proposed new service from Bradford to Haworth. Being displeased with this action, the company immediately lodged an appeal with the Ministry of Transport and this brought a quick

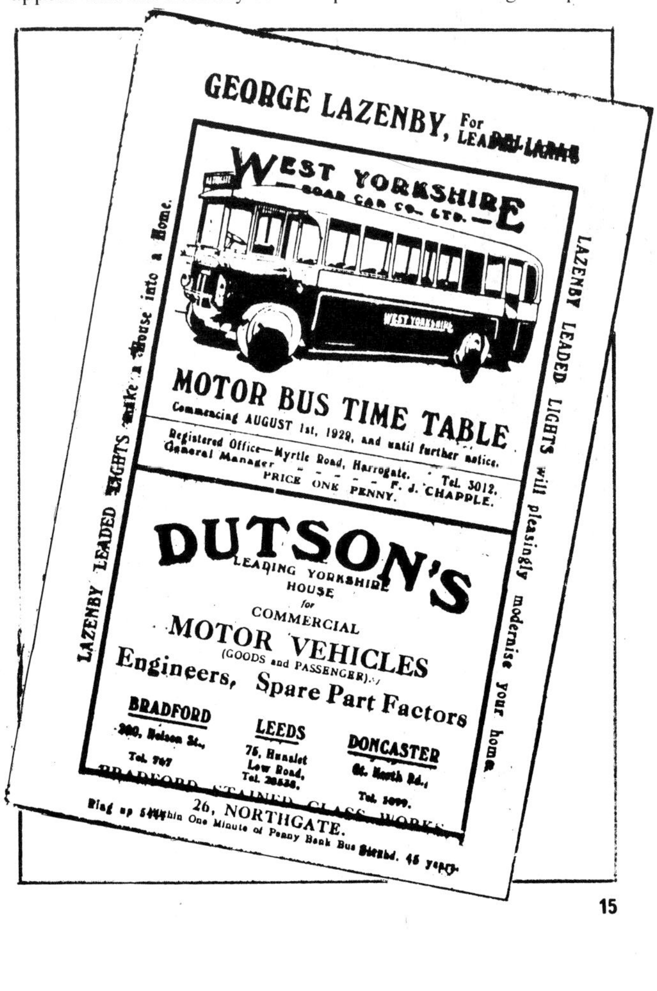

A busy day in August 1928 sees the then brand-new Leyland TD1 402 in Keighley whilst operating the Bradford – Skipton route. Although fleet numbers were allocated, they were not carried on West Yorkshire's vehicles at that time.

change of heart by the U.D.C. who in November granted the required licence and thus allowing West Yorkshire to withdraw their appeal before it was heard.

Following the opening of the first part of the new depot at Hammerton Street, Bradford, the old Edderthorpe Street premises were leased to their former owners, Blythe & Berwick in November 1928 whilst the company's lease on the Wetherby garage, their premises at Chester Street, Bradford and the garage at Otley Road, Shipley were all renewed for a further period. A further plot of land at Roseville Road, Leeds adjacent to the company's new garage was bought in November, as was some land at 76 Wellington Street, Leeds where it was proposed to build a bus station.

Following the resignation on 31 December of Herbert Raworth as Managing Director, a position he had held since April 1907, Francis John Chapple was appointed General Manager, taking up his new office on 1 January 1929. Continuing the pattern set up by his predecessor, it was not long before more independent operators began to be swallowed up by the company. The first to succumb to an offer was F. Murgatroyd of Eldwick, proprietor of Eldwick Motor Services who sold his Bingley to Eldwick service and 3 buses (a Karrier, Morris and Guy) to West Yorkshire on 5 March. Later the same month, on the 23rd., F. Reynard's Lion Bus Service of Easingwold was acquired along with 4 Leyland buses and a Dennis and a service from York to Thirsk. Following on 5 April was Samuel Hawkridge of Wetherby with a mixed fleet of 8 maroon & primrose liveried buses and services from York to Wetherby and York to Scarborough. Next came the business of Hardcastle and Lockwood who operated under the name of Yeadon Transport Co. with a fleet of 15 single deck buses. Taken over on 16 May was their entire fleet; services from Yeadon to Leeds and Bradford and property at Yeadon and Hawksworth. Their Waterside Garage at Yeadon was retained by West Yorkshire as a new operating base, this being temporarily being shared with the house coal delivery business which was retained by Yeadon Transport.

This view shows Reynard's Lion Bus Service PY8292, an N.M.U.-bodied Dennis G-type 20-seat bus when new in 1928. A year later it passed to West Yorkshire along with the Reynard business to become 149 in its new owner's fleet where it remained in service until 1933.

At around this time, the company purchased from Ribble Motor Services the Bolton Abbey to Skipton service which Ribble had acquired from Old Bill Motor Services of Skipton operated by Mr. A. Wiseman, but no vehicles were involved in this deal.

The take over machine rolled on relentlessly and on 4 June the total assets of Strensall Motor Services Ltd. of Strensall, York were acquired. These included 2 Maxwell buses, 3 Dennis' and a Ford; a service from Strensall to York and some property at Strensall. Surprisingly, after an uneventful July, August proved to be a month of months with no fewer than four more companies being acquired. The first was Mr. Ellis' Peoples Motor Service of Haxby, York which brought with it on August 13 two buses (a Thornycroft and a Garner) and a service from York to Haxby. Two days later another York independent passed to the company, this being K. Tanner's Green Bus Service of Acomb with 3 Vulcans and a Dennis and two services, York to Knapton and York to Nether Poppleton. Following on the 21st of the month was the business of Bolton & Wood of Pool in Wharfedale who had just one bus (a 20-seat Vulcan) and a service from Otley to Horsforth. Finally came Red, White & Blue Motor Services Ltd. of Aberford who ran from Leeds to Micklefield and had a fleet of 11 buses, all of which passed to their new owner on 29 August. Although this completed the acquisitions of 1929, it was decided on 25 September to put Keighley Bros (Omnibuses) Ltd. into voluntary liquidation following the transfer of its fleet to West Yorkshire on 1 July.

Keighley Brothers Leyland C9 bus CW6432 pictured here on their York service passed to West Yorkshire in June 1928 when it was allocated fleet number 143.
(The late R. Jackson)

Property too was an important aspect of the company's development and from 1 May temporary depot accommodation

Yeadon Transport 's newest bus was this Ramsden-bodied Leyland TS2 which was delivered only days before the company was taken over by West Yorkshire in May 1929. Numbered 507 by its new owners, it was eventually transferred to Keighley West Yorkshire in 1934.

One of 6 Tilling Stevens B10B charabancs purchased by West Yorkshire in 1928, 154 is seen here wearing its original grey & red livery. Two charas of the identical type were also purchased for the Carriage Co. subsidiary in whose biscuit & tan livery they were delivered.

was taken on a one year lease at Fawcett Street, York. Later in the year it was agreed to purchase a site in Barbican Road, York where a permanent garage could be built whilst in Keighley two more plots of land were bought adjoining the Anvil Street garage and new offices had been leased in Russell Street. The garage at Marley Street, Keighley had now been sub-let to Keighley Corporation Tramways after being vacant for some short time.

The updating of the fleet continued throughout the year and all of the buses ordered in 1928 had by now entered service. Additional orders placed in March, and November between them called for a further 40 Tilling B10A2s, 14 Leyland Titan TD1 double deckers and 15 Leyland Tiger chassis, 10 of which were to be fitted with long distance bodies. Also ordered was an Armstrong Siddeley staff car for the General Manager's use. The size of the 1929 orders allowed not only further expansion, but also enabled 26 buses and 14 charabancs – many of which had been acquired with the various businesses taken over – to be withdrawn and sold. In addition to these, Tilling Stevens agreed in November to buy back 8 of the petrol-electric TS6s purchased in 1924 which were duly withdrawn early in 1930 upon receipt of their replacements.

The first of the Roe-bodied Tiger long distance coaches arrived towards the end of May and as soon as sufficient were received, West Yorkshire inaugurated their new service from Harrogate to London via Leeds, Doncaster, Grantham and Stamford. The first journey on this 220-mile route was made on Friday 19 July 1929 and from thence on, the service operated daily in each direction. This was a prelude to the introduction of numerous other long distance services which were eventually to spread out across Britain and were operated jointly with other undertakings.

Following the opening of the new garage at Grove Park, Harrogate, the former Bilton Motor Co. premises at Mornington Terrace had been used to store old vehicles and sundry equipment. No longer required for this purpose, the property was leased from 1 April to W.S. Ward Ltd. for a five year term with an option to purchase the garage and two houses at any time during the first three years. Meanwhile the new bus station at Wellington Street, Leeds was now fully operational and provided a source of revenue from the fees charged to other operators using this site.

Returning momentarily to the fleet, it is interesting to note that West Yorkshire and Chas. H. Roe (who built the bodies for the Leyland Tiger long distance coaches) had between them developed a new luggage carrier and ventilator device which was tested on these vehicles. Such was its success that the device was jointly patented by the two companies in November 1929.

A further feature adopted by West Yorkshire in 1929 was the 'bible' destination indicator – a fitting which was to be characteristic for almost a quarter of a century. Heavy metal boards, vertically hinged in their centre to enable different destinations to be displayed by 'turning the pages', these were carried in frames in place of the more conventional roller blind indicators. The first vehicles delivered new with 'bible' equipment were the Roe-bodied Leyland TS1 coaches which made their debut in May and during the following year or so, all the other vehicles in the fleet were similarly fitted.

An unusual acquisition made in November 1929 was that of Scarborough & District Motor Services Ltd. of Scarborough who was jointly bought by West Yorkshire, United and East Yorkshire. The division of the company gave West Yorkshire a service from York to Scarborough and provided them with an additional 9 buses (5 Albions, 2 GMCs and 2 Leylands), although the transaction was not completed until May 1930.

1930 saw even greater changes within the company, especially as far as the fleet was concerned. Unlike previous years, the bodywork order for the new Tilling B10A2s was shared between three coachbuilders rather than being placed solely with Tilling. 20 of the bodies were to be built at the Lowestoft factory of United Automobile Services, 10 were allocated to Tilling and the

One of the tiny 14-seat Bean buses, 109, is seen here on the Laycock service in 1927 whilst owned by West Yorkshire's subsidiary, Premier of Keighley.

511, a Roe-bodied Leyland TS2 coach spent much of its early life operating the prestige service from Harrogate to London. Unusually it is seen here minus its roof-mounted side destination boards.

One of a pair of Tilling-bodied B10As delivered to Harrogate Carriage Co. in 1928, WW4259 is pictured here wearing its owner's attractive biscuit & tan livery complete with scroll-type fleet name.

remaining ten were to be bodied locally by Chas. H. Roe of Leeds. All the bodies were however to be built to similar design, although quite naturally many of the distinguishing features of each individual builder were incorporated. New orders placed were for 15 Leyland TD1 double deckers with Leyland open staircase bodywork; 10 Tilling Stevens B10A2 single deckers and a Jowett staff car and in April approval was given to purchase a Dennis omnibus, although in the event this was never ordered. A further 20 Leyland Tigers were also ordered and in November a secondhand Armstrong Siddeley Landaulette was acquired from Thomas Tilling Ltd., London.

Following negotiations entered into in July 1929 with the London North Eastern and London Midland & Scottish Railway Companies, both these undertakings jointly acquired a substantial financial interest (equal to that of Tilling & B.A.T.) in West Yorkshire Road Car and also entered into working agreements from 1 January with the object of co-ordinating road and rail services in the area served by the company. One of the first proposals made under this agreement was the proposed closing of the Skipton – Grassington railway line (LMS) and the provision of a replacement bus service, half the profits from which would be payable to the railway company should the closure take place. Other similar proposals were made during the years ahead, some of which were found acceptable, others which were rejected.

A further proposal put by the LMS and LNE Railway companies related to Hebble Bus Services of Halifax whom they had purchased in 1929 from O. & C. Holdsworth (who had a decade earlier started Bilton Motor Co. at Harrogate). This was offered to Yorkshire (WD) Electric Tramways and West Yorkshire in the proportions of 75% and 25% respectively and the company decided to take up this offer. After protracted negotiations, it was agreed in July not to proceed in view of other pending developments and the talks were never reopened. At this same time (March 1930) Keighley Corporation Tramways invited West Yorkshire to make an offer for the purchase or the management on their behalf of the Corporation's tramway undertaking and this proved far more attractive to West Yorkshire than the Hebble deal. Talks began at once and as will be seen later, were finally concluded in 1932.

The purchase of smaller operators within the company's territory continued unabated and on 10 January Hedna Bus Service of Eccleshill, Bradford was acquired from A.R. Robinson. This added 4 Guys and 4 Leylands to the West Yorkshire fleet together with services from Bradford to Leeds via Greengates and Bradford to Yeadon. Universal Motors (Leeds) Ltd. of Thorner followed on 22 March bringing a service from Leeds to Thorner and 3 buses (2 Karriers and a Chevrolet) whilst during the following month Chapman of Grassington and part of Ebor Trading Co., York were taken over. The Chapman

Tilling Stevens B10A 234 is pictured in Keighley in 1928 whilst working the Oakworth route.

Left: 622, a 25-seat Star Flyer taken over with the Chapman, Grassington business in 1930 rests in Grassington Market Place before its rural run to Skipton.

business dated back to 1883 when Christopher Chapman obtained the mail contract from Skipton to Buckden, high in the Yorkshire Dales. The mail contract had been retained since that date and passed to West Yorkshire upon the acquisition of the Chapman business on 11 April. Services transferred to the company were from Skipton to Buckden; Skipton to Hawes and Leyburn and Grassington to Ilkley and 11 buses and charabancs were also included in the deal as was a garage at Grassington. Ebor Trading Co. of York was bought jointly with United on 12 April, West Yorkshire's share being 4 Dennis buses and a service from York to Malton via the villages enroute.

Pictured when new, Wharfedale Motors Alexander-bodied Crossley Eagle WW8692 was new in 1929. Passing to West Yorkshire with the Wharfedale business in June 1930, this 32-seat bus continued in service with its new owner until the end of 1935.

KH4786, an all-Albion PK26 bus of 1927 vintage passed to West Yorkshire three years later with the Cosy Car Service business of Haxby, York. Withdrawn from service in October 1933 it was sold to a Scottish dealer and later saw further service in Ayrshire.

Before the summer was over, three more independent operators were to fall to the might of West Yorkshire, the first of which was E. Nelson's Skipton-based Wharfedale Motors Ltd. who operated a fleet of 9 buses on Dales services from Skipton to Buckden; Litton and Skyreholme. Just one day later West Yorkshire took over the operations and buses of W. Mennell (Cosy Car Services), York who ran from York to Wiggington (the scene of the battle for York in 1986) and had a fleet of 6 vehicles. Moving back to the Yorkshire Dales, on 27 July the bus operations of Longster Bros., Pateley Bridge were acquired, these comprising services radiating from Pateley Bridge to Summerbridge; Middlesmoor and Greenhow and 4 small buses, all of which were of different makes (Guy, Bean, Crossley and Vulcan).

There was now a slight respite before any more acquisitions were undertaken and during this time West Yorkshire purchased shares in London Coastal Coaches Ltd. During September a 10-year lease was taken on part of the station yard at Pateley Bridge owned by the LNE Railway and it was decided to remove to this site one of the sectional garages already owned by the company to provide undercover accommodation for the buses kept in the town. Earlier in the year (in March) West Yorkshire had sold the property they owned at Strensall and Nelson Road, Ilkley as it was felt that this was no longer needed.

The final expansion of 1930 came when two more companies were purchased, one in York, the other in Bradford. In York, on 15 October, the company bought from United Automobile Services the York – Copmanthorpe, York – Walshford Bridge and York – Nun Monkton services formerly operated by Ovington Motors Ltd. together with 4 buses whilst in Bradford on 20 November the stage carriage services from Bradford to Grassington and Bradford to Scarborough of J.W. North Ltd. were acquired along with 13 coaches. J.W. North retained his coaching and haulage parts of his business, eventually selling the former to Wallace Arnold Tours, Leeds in 1936 and continuing to operate his lorries until nationalisation in 1948.

The fleet was now changing rapidly with an assortment of non-standard makes being acquired with the companies taken over, the delivery of new vehicles continuing and the withdrawal of a large number of now obsolete and time expired machines. A total of 43 old vehicles were disposed of during 1931 and before the end of the year authorisation was given for the sale of a further 41 as soon as their replacements arrived in 1932. Orders for new buses continued to be placed in quantity and during 1931 no fewer than 30 T.S. Motors B49A7 single deckers were requested together with 30 Eastern Counties Coach Works bodies. Additionally, 5 secondhand Tilling Stevens B9A chassis were purchased from Thomas Tilling Ltd., these being fitted with new United bodies before their delivery to Harrogate during May. An addition to the service fleet was a Jowett van which was to be used by the company's publicity department.

In consideration of their future vehicle policy, it was decided in May to hire two chassis embodying certain improvements from the Daimler Co. Ltd. and T.S. Motors Ltd. The Daimler, a CH6

Although delivered with a roller blind front destination indicator, 1930 Leyland TD1 428 quickly gained a typical West Yorkshire bible desty as seen in this 1931 view at Thirsk Row, Leeds. (Leyland)

Above: 516, one of a batch of 5 Roe-bodied Leyland TS2 buses bought new in 1930.

Left: Enroute to Hawes, high in the Yorkshire Dales, 519, the Leyland TS1 bought from Midland Red in 1930 is followed by 233, one of the 1928 Tilling Stevens B10A buses.

with Roe 34-seat front entrance bodywork arrived in July and was immediately placed in service on a variety of routes to evaluate it against other members of the fleet. Spending all of its life with the company running from Harrogate depot (due to its close proximity with the central workshops at Myrtle Road), it continued to be used until the end of August 1937, being returned to its owners some twelve months later. The T.S. Motors chassis was an E60A6 model with 6-cylinder engine and Charles Roberts 34-seat body. This arrived at Harrogate on 25 September and was used in service until the beginning of October 1932 when it was returned to its owner's Maidstone factory. Although proving reasonably successful during their trials, chassis of neither type were ever ordered as the company decided to keep with the Tilling policy of that time.

In addition to the two buses taken into stock for evaluation, the company also undertook some experimental work of their own in 1932 when they adapted one of their Tilling B10As to run on creosote oil. After a few months, this bus (231) reverted to its more conventional petrol propulsion.

During January 1931 the property at Chester Street, Bradford previously leased from Childe & Co. Ltd was purchased, as were 2 houses adjoining this site and during the next five years, all the remaining property in Chester Street together with some in Wilton Street and Little Horton Lane was acquired to enable a bus station to be built on this site. Further property was also gained adjoining the Myrtle Road workshops at Harrogate and a further house in East Parade was added to the company's development plan. Seeking offices in Skipton, West Yorkshire took the lease of two rooms at Ship Buildings, Swadford Street whilst back in Harrogate it was decided to give up the separate Carriage Company office at 33 Montpellier Parade and merge the private hire department into the company's nearby offices at 28 Montpellier Parade. Following the expiry of the lease of the garage at Edderthorpe Street, Bradford to Blythe & Berwick, it was agreed to rent this building to Yorkshire (W.D.) Electric Tramways Ltd. for a three year period commencing in May. Two months later, notice of termination of the tenancy agreement for the portion of the Wetherby garage taken over from S.

Two single deckers were taken into stock in 1931 for evaluation purposes. One of these was Roe-bodied Daimler CH6 WX8098 which was given fleet number 656. It remained in service until 1938.

The other bus hired for evaluation in 1931 was 657 (KJ2914), a Charles Roberts-bodied T.S. Motors E60A6 34-seater. This had a comparatively short life with West Yorkshire, being returned to its owners in October 1932 after which it was rebuilt as a double decker for Westcliff-on-Sea Motor Services.

The final batch of Tilling B10A2s to be purchased arrived in 1931 and carried United 30-seat bodywork. This veiw shows 710 specially posed for the official photographer on the Stray at Harrogate when new.

The first double deckers to be purchased with enclosed staircases were the 1932 Leyland TD2s. 435 seen here at Silsden on the Ilkley – Keighley service was sold to Keighley Corporation when only three months old and passed to the newly-formed Keighley West Yorkshire a few days later. (The late R. Jackson)

Hawkridge Ltd. was given and at this same time part of the Waterside Garage at Yeadon was leased to the Waterside Boot Manufacturing Co. (1930) Ltd. Finally, in November the Shipley garage was sold to Mr. E.B. Watkin, the vehicles allocated to that depot being transferred to Bradford.

Before the end of the year, West Yorkshire increased their share holding in London Coastal Coaches Ltd. and also signed an agreement with United for the joint use of the latter's bus station at Valley Bridge, Scarborough.

A surprise purchase on 27 June was that of a three-year old Leyland Tiger TS1 bus from Midland Red of Birmingham. The reason for this acquisition is not known, although perhaps it was considered non-standard by the Birmingham company as it had only survived for one month in their ownership after having been acquired by them from the G.W.R. Road Motor Division.

Only one operator was acquired during 1931, this being H. Dodsworth & Sons of Minskip who on 11 April sold the stage carriage part of his business with routes from Harrogate to Boroughbridge and Knaresborough to Great Ouseburn to the company along with 2 Chevrolets and a Ford. Dodsworth retained his coaching interests which are still operated by his family today.

By the turn of the year, agreement had been reached with Keighley Corporation for the setting up of a joint board subject to the settlement of certain details as to the method of operation and after approval had been given by the Council it was hoped to commence the new arrangement on 1 January 1932. This was not to be however due to the delay in gaining approval from the Ministry of Transport and it was to be later in the year before the joint agreement could be implemented. Meanwhile the lease of the garage in Marley Street, Keighley expired on 1 February and this was not renewed. A proposal was put forward in connection with the extension of the garage at Anvil Street in the town where it was agreed to include a forecourt.

Not far away in Skipton, during the summer the purchase of the Craven Arms with land at the rear and two shops adjoining was undertaken so that a garage joint with Ribble could be built at the back of the hotel. At Harrogate, thoughts were turned to the construction of a new head office and a new body shop on land owned in East Parade and it was agreed to start work on both at the earliest possible opportunity. At the other side of the town, the lease of the garage at the White Hart Hotel was extended for a further year from 1 November and this continued to be used for the housing of the company's private hire fleet.

Whilst awaiting the outcome of the Ministry of Transport's deliberations on the new Keighley operation, the company opened talks with York Corporation in an attempt to obtain a similar agreement to that reached with Keighley. These were rather more complicated however and were to continue on and off for two more years before a final conclusion was reached. At this same time arrangements were entered into with Bradford Corporation for co-ordinating services on the Bankfoot – Park Gates route. The proposal for the company to withdraw from their Bradford – Clayton service inherited from Blythe & Berwick in exchange for the Corporation withdrawing their trackless trolleybuses on the Canal Road route was also discussed and agreement was reached that this should be undertaken as quickly as was practicable.

The fleet was once again updated by the addition of a large number of new buses with the arrival of the 30 T.S. Motors B49A7s; 6 Leyland Tiger TS4 long distance coaches; and a Dennis Lancet I which had been ordered at the start of 1932 for evaluation purposes. Arriving in June were a batch of 6 Leyland

With its outward-hinged door open, 1932 ECOC-bodied Leyland TS4 coach 544 is pictured here operating the Hull-Liverpool limited stop service in pre-war days. (G. H. F. Atkins)

735, one of the then-new ECOC-bodied T. S. Motors B49A7s picks up its Harrogate-bound passengers at Ilkley railway station in August 1932. Duplicating it on this busy summer's day is 44, a Tilling Stevens B9A of 1927 vintage.
(The late R. Jackson)

TD2s, the company's first enclosed staircase double deckers which had only been ordered some three months earlier. All the buses and coaches delivered during 1932 had bodywork by E.C.O.C., thus maintaining Tilling group policy.

In order to extend the lives of 20 of the Tilling Stevens B9As which had entered the fleet during the 1926/7 period, these were despatched to Lowestoft for fitting with new E.C.O.C. bodies and later in the year it was decided to treat the remaining 25 B9As similarly. Two new Morris staff cars were bought to replace an older car of the same make and a Bean and in October an order was placed for a further 42 T.S. Motors B49A7 single deckers and 6 Leyland Tiger TS4s for delivery in 1933. Also authorised was the re-seating of 6 of the Leyland Tiger buses at a cost of £150 each. On the debit side, 24 obsolete vehicles were sold at the start of the year to a dealer at Huddersfield.

At the start of the summer, joint services with Ribble commenced between Leeds and Blackpool, Leeds and Morecambe, Leeds and Keswick and from Liverpool to Scarborough.

Apart from the Keighley agreement, of which more later, the only operators to be taken over during 1932 were the omnibus portion of George Deverew of Haxby, York on 26 February with services from York to Flaxton and Warthill and on 27 April the goodwill and Skipton – Connonley route of H. W. Ratcliffe's Connonley Motors Ltd. On neither occasion were any vehicles taken over, the services being easily maintained with buses from the company's own fleet.

CONTROL GAINED AT KEIGHLEY

At last the agreement with Keighley Corporation was finally signed and on 2 October the new Keighley West Yorkshire Services began operating. Prior to this, the Corporation had abandoned their trolleybus system on 31 August and had borrowed five West Yorkshire Titan TD2s to maintain the services during the interim period. In addition, in order to adjust the financial structure of the Corporation prior to the launching of the new joint company, one of West Yorkshire's recently-delivered TD2s was purchased on 1 September. Registered on 2 September with a nominal share capital of £1,000 in £1 shares held by both parties, the head office of the new company was at Myrtle Road, Harrogate in the headquarters of West Yorkshire Road Car Co. Ltd.

Thirteen Corporation routes and eight West Yorkshire services within the Keighley area were transferred to the new joint company to which the Corporation contributed 31 buses and West Yorkshire transferred 27. The latter were a mixture of Leyland and Guy single deckers acquired from various independent operators taken over in previous years, some elderly Tilling Stevens and 7 Leyland TD1s. Additionally 5 Leyland TD2s and 3 single deckers (a Star, Dennis and Leyland) were hired to the new undertaking for a number of months until new vehicles on order arrived. The first of these were a batch of 7 E.C.O.C.-bodied TD2s which took up their duties during

Keighley Corporation withdrew the last of their trolleybuses on 31 August 1932, a month before the formation of Keighley West Yorkshire and thus the new undertaking never operated electric traction. One of the Brush-bodied Straker trolleybuses is seen here turning at Stockbridge in Corporation days.
(The late R. Jackson)

A busy scene in Cooke Street, Keighley shows a variety of West Yorkshire and Keighley Corporation buses and a Keighley trolleybus enroute to Stockbridge in 1931.

Keighley Corporation 34, a Leyland C9 of 1925 vintage which later became Keighley West Yorkshire K664 is seen climbing Thwaites Brow in the winter snow of 1927.

Inherited from Keighley Corporation upon the formation of the new joint undertaking in 1932 was Leyland Lioness WW1880 (K191) seen here battling with winter weather conditions in 1933.

December. These were joined in March 1933 by a pair of E.C.O.C.-bodied Leyland forward control Cub 24-seaters which were required for service on the Riddlesden route which passed over a light bridge across the Leeds & Liverpool canal before reaching its terminus.

Returning to West Yorkshire Road Car Co., the company sold 10 of their Leyland PLSC Lion buses to Jersey Motor Transport in November with a further 6 following in May 1933. 20 more buses were sold at the start of 1933 and 6 more went before the end of the year. At a meeting on 1 February 1933 it was decided not to purchase the 42 T.S. Motors B49A7s ordered the previous year after all but instead to buy 22 Dennis Lancet Is and to defer the remaining 20 for the time being. These were eventually confirmed in July as being Lancet Is and all 42 were to have E.C.O.C. 34-seat bodywork. The first of these arrived in June and delivery was completed before the end of the year. Two additional staff cars were also taken into stock, these being a Lanchester and a Wolseley, both of which were bought new.

The acquisition of further businesses continued and on 21 March the whole of the issued share capital of the Fawdon Omnibus Co. Ltd. of Newcastle upon Tyne was bought on behalf of the companies operating the Liverpool – Newcastle service and Yorkshire Services Pool services, West Yorkshire's share was to be one quarter of the total, the other three quarters passing to Northern General; Yorkshire (W.D.) Electric Tramways and Yorkshire Traction. On the same day, the business of Hale Garage & Coachways Ltd. of London was purchased on behalf of the members of the Yorkshire Services Pool and again West Yorkshire's share was one quarter. On the latter occasion, West Yorkshire also inherited a Brush-bodied Dennis E-type bus with their share, this carrying a secondhand 31-seat centre-entrance body.

On 19 July yet another joint purchase was made, when W. Armitage & Sons Ltd. of Blackpool was acquired by the five associated companies forming the Yorkshire-Blackpool Pool. West Yorkshire's share was 28½% on this occasion, just as it was when on 20 September the share capital of Walker Taylor Sons Ltd. of Blackpool was obtained by the 5 associated companies. With the Walker Taylor share, the company gained 3 Tilling Stevens coaches and a Leyland Cub.

Next followed W. M. Suddaby & Sons of Malton which, although outside the company's main operating area was purchased on 20 September in agreement with United. The Suddaby business gave West Yorkshire a rural service from Malton to Gilling and added a further 6 vehicles to the fleet, although only 2 of these were operated, the other 4 being resold immediately.

Finally, November brought with it interest in three more companies. Firstly on the 18th of the month Tyne & Mersey Motor Services Ltd. of Newcastle upon Tyne was acquired by 6 associated companies and then divided proportionately with West Yorkshire gaining a 17% share. On the following day United, who had just purchased the Leeds & Newcastle Omnibus Co. Ltd. of Northallerton agreed to sell to members of the Northern Pool such parts of the business as was concerned with the operation of the service between Leeds and Newcastle via Ripon, Thirsk and Northallerton. West Yorkshire's share of the company included 8 vehicles, although these were resold to other members of the Pool without being taken into stock.

The last of the three November acquisitions took place on the 22nd of the month and concerned the Tadcaster independent, Corcoran Bros. Ltd. who ran services from Leeds to York and

West Yorkshire built up a large fleet of ECOC-bodied Dennis Lancet Is between 1932 and 1935. 831, a 1933 example is seen here in Harrogate bus station whilst working a local town service. This bus had a comparatively short life, being withdrawn in 1939 and then stored until sold nine years later.

Corcoran Bros. bought this Albion PMB28 in 1930. Passing to West Yorkshire three years later with the Corcoran business, it is seen here in 1932 in Leeds whilst operating on its owner's Scarborough service.

Scarborough, from York to Malton; Wighill; Bramham and Pontefract. Their yellow & black liveried fleet of 3 Albions, 5 Leylands and 13 AECs was transferred to its new owner in its entirity and many of these vehicles continued to operate for West Yorkshire until as late as 1950.

On the property scene, the erection of the new body shop at the central repair works in Harrogate had been completed during April and work on the building of the new head office was at an advanced stage. The resale of the company's Keighley premises to the newly formed Keighley West Yorkshire undertaking was undertaken during September and a month later construction of the new garage at Skipton began. In Leeds, some land and buildings in Vicar Lane and New York Road which had been offered to the company were purchased with a view to providing a bus station on this site at some future time. A further one-year lease on the White Hart Hotel garage at Harrogate was signed on 1 November, thus continuing its use as a garage for the private hire fleet for yet another twelve months.

1933 ended on a sad note with the death of West Yorkshire's founder, Herbert Raworth on 27 December. He was the gentleman who had successfully steered the company from its outset in 1906 and who had been at the helm for so many years. Without his foresight, determination and expertise the company would not have survived its first decade, let alone survive for over a quarter of a century to become an important operator not only in Harrogate, but throughout West Yorkshire.

The new year began with a minor disaster when Armstrong Siddeley staff car WX3 was destroyed by fire and a replacement in the form of a Morris Minor had to be purchased. Orders were placed in January for 20 more Dennis Lancet I single deckers and for 6 little Dennis Ace 20-seaters all with E.C.O.C. bodywork and in addition, 13 new Northern Counties single deck bodies were contracted for fitting to Albion PMA28-type chassis

The need for small capacity vehicles for operation on the Keighley – Morton – Bingley service can be clearly seen as Keighley West Yorkshire E.C.O.C.-bodied Leyland Cub K673 crosses one of the swing bridges over the Leeds – Liverpool canal.
(Leyland)

Looking immaculate and wearing its owner's Yorkshire Rose symbol in place of a more conventional fleet name. ECOC-bodied Leyland TS4 549 new in 1933 is seen here operating the Harrogate – Birmingham limited stop service. Its roof-mounted luggage carrier was removed later in life after 549 was relegated to stage carriage duties.
(G. H. F. Atkins)

The lavishly-appointed Board Room at the company's new head office in East Parade, Harrogate was panelled with polished wood and boasted an ornate glass-windowed roof.

A line-up of N.C.M.E.-rebodied Albion PMA28s at Grove Park depot, Harrogate in 1938 shows from left to right 5, 8, 6, 10, 13, 9, 12, 7, 11 and 2. It is interesting to note that each of these buses carries a rear advert for electricity.

Resting in Harrogate bus station in 1938 is Dennis Ace 611, one of a trio delivered to the combined fleets in 1937. Its 20-seat body is by E.C.W.

already owned by the company after these had been overhauled at Myrtle Road. A further order placed in September called for the company's first Bristol chassis – 20 JO5Gs and 13 GO5Gs together with a further 18 Lancet Is and another 2 Dennis Aces. 50 obsolete vehicles were sold in three different batches plus a further two which were disposed of individually.

During the summer, a start was made on the extension to the company's Grove Park garage at Harrogate and to Roseville Road garage at Leeds and in March, some freehold property at 8 Market Street, Skipton was bought. Further property was purchased in Bradford at Little Horton Lane and Wilton Street and consideration was given to three more pieces of land in Vicar Lane, Leeds which were ultimately purchased in January 1935. More unusually, a site of some 5480 sq.yds. known as 'The Belvedere' with buildings thereon in Victoria Avenue, Harrogate was acquired in November, although the company had no immediate plans for its use. The garage at Eldwick acquired with the Eldwick Motor Services and had been unused since 1929 was leased to J. R. Hardcastle towards the end of the year and was later sold to this person.

JOINT OWNERSHIP AT YORK

1934 proved to be the last year of major expansion in the pre-war period, but what expansion there was. After two years of negotiation, agreement was at last reached with York Corporation for the formation of a Joint Committee which would be responsible for the operation of all the Corporation's and company's services in this ancient city. Although York-West Yorkshire had already been documented in detail in the book 'York City Buses' published by Autobus Review Publications in 1984, it is worthy of note that the formation of the Joint Committee took place on 1 April for a minimum period of 21 years and that all profits or losses during that period of time would be equally shared between the Corporation and West

York Corporation trolleybus no.30 makes its way to Heworth in pre-York West Yorkshire days. A Karrier Clough E4, it had Roe rear-entrance bodywork.

York Corporation 42, one of the cars bought from Burton on Trent in 1930 stands opposite the railway station on its way to Acomb.

Former York Corporation Leyland LT2 Y660 rests opposite the railway station in company with a highbridge Bristol GO5G and an ex.West Yorkshire Leyland TD1 in York West Yorkshire days in 1938.

Yorkshire. When the new undertaking came into being on 1 April, York Corporation were still operating a fleet of 45 tramcars along with 3 single deck trolleybuses and 21 single deck and 3 double deck motor buses. All of these were transferred to the new joint body together with 27 buses from the West Yorkshire fleet. The latter comprised Tilling Stevens B9As and B10A2s, Leyland PLSC Lions and 5 Dennis Lancet Is. All these along with the former Corporation motor buses were given a 'Y' prefix to their fleet numbers to signify that they were York-West Yorkshire vehicles just as those in the Keighley West Yorkshire fleet had received a 'K' prefix in 1932. Although the company were now responsible for trams and trolleybuses for the first time in their history, their excursion into the world of electric traction was to be but a short one. The last of the trams made their final journeys on Saturday 16 November 1935 whilst the three trolleybuses suffered this fate even earlier, being withdrawn on 6 January of that year. To compensate for the loss of the trams, 5 Leyland open staircase TD1s were transferred from West Yorkshire to the York fleet in March 1935 with a further 7 making this same move some eight months later. All the Corporation's motor buses were immediately transferred from their former garage at Fulford to West Yorkshire's Barbican Road premises, leaving only the trams and trolleybuses working from the Corporation garage until their final demise.

Seen early in 1934 shortly before being transferred to York-West Yorkshire, West Yorkshire Road Car Co. Ltd. Tilling Stevens B10A2 single decker 243 prepares to leave Barbican Road depot for a spell of service. (C. W. Routh collection)

During September an agreement was reached with J. Bullock & Sons (1928) Ltd. of Featherstone for an exchange of services to give each operator routes within their own operating areas. In this deal West Yorkshire's ex.Corcoran route from Tadcaster to Pontefract passed to J. Bullock & Sons who in turn handed their Tadcaster – Haxby service to the company. The exchange did not become effective until 25 November and almost immediately the York – Haxby section of this route was transferred to the York-West Yorkshire undertaking. A more important transaction undertaken during September was the purchase by West Yorkshire on behalf of the members of the Yorkshire Services Pool of London, Midland & Yorkshire Services Ltd., of which the company's share was to be 22%. Two months later, United Automobile Services who had acquired Phillipsons Motor Coaches Ltd. of Kings Cross, London agreed to sell to members of the Yorkshire Services Pool parts of the service from Scarborough to London and with West Yorkshire's share came 2 Gilford coaches. Some weeks earlier, on 26 October West Yorkshire gained further consolidation of their interests in the York area when they purchased the goodwill and omnibus portion of the business of W. Craven of Terrington. Although no vehicles were taken over, this gave them a service from York to Shackleton to the north of the city. Finally, in July the company acquired 5,000 shares in the newly formed Blackpool Omnibus Stations Ltd.

Across in Keighley 1934 saw the purchase by Keighley West Yorkshire of one half of E. Laycock's interest in the Keighley Colne service, the other half of which passed to Burnley, Colne & Nelson Joint Committee. This took the joint undertaking's buses across the border into Lancashire for the first time on this shared service. The new buses added to the fleet during the year brought a number of surprises. First came four double deckers on 6 June. Two were Leyland TD2s – the last of this type to be built, the TD2 having been superceded by the more modern TD3

The first Bristol double deckers to be purchased were a pair of Brush lowbridge-bodied GO5Gs which joined the Keighley West Yorkshire fleet in 1934. The second of these, K112 (later renumbered K302) is seen here when new.
(Brush, courtesy of Leicester Museums).

model a year earlier – and even more unusual, these were fitted with Gardner 5LW oil engines unlike all the previous TD2s which had been petrol engined. Fitted with E.C.O.C. lowbridge bodies of almost identical styling to those delivered in 1932, they looked somewhat old fashioned in their appearance right from the start. The other two new double deckers were equally as unusual being the company's first Bristols. Of the G-type, these had been built as petrol engined chassis but had been altered to Gardner 5LW diesel before completion and thus had become Bristol's first oil-engined deckers. Their lowbridge bodies were built by Brush rather than by E.C.O.C. and seating was provided for 52-passengers. Finally came a pair of 20-seat E.C.O.C.-bodied Dennis Aces which made their first appearance on 5 December. Also added to the fleet during the year were two Leyland TS1s transferred from West Yorkshire on 1 April.

1935 began with plans being submitted for a new bus station at Chester Street, Bradford and following their approval a start was made on the demolition of the company-owned property on the west side of the site. This eventually came into use in its new capacity during the final month of the year and was at first used solely by the company's own vehicles. In March further land was bought adjacent to the garage at Barbican Road, York and additionally a small plot was purchased in New Brook Street, Ilkley with a view to building a bus station at some future date if this was thought desirable. Later in the year, in July the company began negotiations with the LNE Railway company for the purchase of some land alongside the railway station at Harrogate and after a conclusion had been reached, Harrogate Corporation gave approval in September for a new bus station to be built on this site. Meanwhile at Leeds, the bus station site at Vicar Lane was being cleared of all its old property in preparation for its new role.

Expansion, albeit in a more modest way, continued and on 16 January the omnibus portion of the business of A. E. Keeling & Sons of Leeds was acquired, providing the company with services from Leeds to Whitby and Leeds to Blackpool. No vehicles were included in the deal however, these being retained by Keeling for the continuation of his private hire business. During 1934 Yorkshire Traction acquired the businesses of Lancashire & Yorkshire Motors of Shafton; Edward Mills Ltd. of Barnsley and Albert Bentley of Barnsley, all of whom operated services to Blackpool. These were then divided amongst the members of the Blackpool Services Pool in July 1935 when West Yorkshire gained a 27% share.

At a meeting held on 26 March, it was decided that there was no necessity to keep Harrogate Carriage Co. Ltd. as a separate subsidiary and it was agreed that it should be put into voluntary liquidation. This was ratified by the Carriage Co. share holders on 4 April after which the wheels were put in motion. Carriage Co's 10 vehicles were moved across to the main West Yorkshire fleet and the actual date of the dissolution of the company was 10

Above: 118, one of the 1934 ECOC-bodied Dennis Ace buses is seen here a year later decorated for the celebrations of King George VIs Silver Jubilee. In 1937 this bus was renumbered 606 and was converted into a depot van in 1941.

Right: Numerically the first of the 1936 ECOC-bodied Bristol J05Gs, 921 is seen here in pre-war days carrying its original livery and working the Leeds – Scarborough service. Note its roof-mounted side destination board holders which were rarely used on stage carriage during the late 'thirties.
(G. H. F. Atkins)

The first Bristol G05Gs for the main company fleet arrived in 1935. 305 pictured here in Bradford's Chester Street bus station was delivered in an experimental livery which incorporated red window frames.

688, a 1931 AEC Regal acquired with the Corcoran business was fitted with new ECOC coach bodywork in 1936. Seen here during its final year in service in 1950, it has been relegated to bus duties and carries its fleet name in equal-sized letters, a style which was to be revived some ten years later.

October 1935.

The fleet itself saw many new arrivals and changes during the year with the delivery of 18 new Dennis Lancet Is; 20 Bristol JO5Gs and 23 Bristol GO5G lowbridge double deckers. The first 13 GO5Gs differed from the remaining 10 in having 5-bay E.C.O.C. bodywork instead of the more customary 6-bay styling, but otherwise were almost identical in their appearance. The JO5Gs all had E.C.O.C. bodywork to West Yorkshire's standard 32-seat front entrance design. During the early part of the year 6 of the ex.Corcoran AEC Regals had their old Craven bodies removed and after undergoing a complete overhaul, their chassis were despatched to Lowestoft where new, luxurious 29-seat coach bodies were fitted. Returning to Harrogate in June, these updated coaches were immediately put to use on the London service where they proved extremely popular with passengers and crews alike.

Orders placed in August for delivery the following year called for 20 oil-engined Dennis Lancet single deckers; 20 Bristol JO5Gs and 10 Bristol GO5Gs, the latter having already been mentioned (the 6-bay variants delivered in November). Also ordered at this same time were 18 coach bodies from E.C.O.C. to replace the old bodies on 18 Leyland Tigers already owned by the company and 1 additional Dennis Lancet oil-engined chassis with an all-metal body built by Chas. H. Roe for trial purposes. This order was however altered in October when the number of JO5Gs was reduced from 20 to 16 and that instead of the 20 oil-engined Dennis chassis, a similar number of Bristol JO5Gs would be purchased. A secondhand Daimler saloon car was also bought during October, as was a Morris Minor car for use by the road inspector. 38 obsolete buses were sold during the year as was the Dodge private hire car.

The York and Keighley fleets also gained a number of new buses in 1935. York in addition to receiving the secondhand TD1s from West Yorkshire also gained 15 new Bristol GO5Gs with E.C.O.C. highbridge bodywork for tramway replacement purposes. Keighley also received a pair of GO5Gs, albeit with lowbridge bodies (one of which did not enter service until 1 January 1936) together with 4 Bristol JO5G single deckers diverted from the West Yorkshire order.

Francis John Chapple relinquished his position of General Manager on 20 November when he left the company to take up a similar post with Bristol Tramways & Carriage Co., his replacement from the first day of that same month being John C. Dean.

York West Yorkshire's first new buses were a batch of 15 highbridge E.C.O.C.-bodied Bristol GO5Gs which took up their duties in 1935. Y318 is seen here in post-war years at the railway station whilst working local town service 2 to Acomb.

The second batch of lowbridge ECOC-bodied Bristol G05Gs carried the more conventional 6-bay type of bodywork. The last example to operate for West Yorkshire was 336 which is seen here on its final day in service, 28 September 1952. Its body was originally fitted to K342 and was transferred to 336 in 1950 after it overturned at Harewood. (J. Copland)

One of the first developments of 1936 was the purchase in February of some land and buildings at the Market Place, Wetherby for use as a bus garage. Some three months later, work began on the demolition of property on the east side of Chester Street, Bradford to enable accommodation to be provided for vehicles of associated companies and others who now wished to use the bus station.

In February, agreement was reached with Bradford Corporation with regard to the company's share of the Lister Park – Bankfoot passing to the Corporation in exchange for the withdrawal of their tram service to Baildon Bridge. At the same time the Harrogate operator, Seanor & Co. who operated excursions from the town and also operated an express service from Harrogate to Blackpool jointly with W. Pyne & Sons of Starbeck was purchased by the company. Part of the cost of this acquisition was borne by other members of the Yorkshire-Blackpool Pool in respect of the half share of the express service. None of the 5 Seanor coaches which passed to West Yorkshire were operated by their new owner.

Orders placed in April for the following year called for no fewer than 45 Bristol JO5Gs, 2 Dennis Aces and 3 Dennis Lancets with Gardner oil engines, and to make way for these, authorisation was given for the disposal of 51 vehicles as and when these were withdrawn. On the non-PSV side, a new Morris saloon staff car was purchased in June.

Amongst the new buses to join the fleet during 1936 was the prototype Dennis Lancet II with all-metal Roe body. Although this did not make its debut until May, it had been exhibited at the Commercial Motor Show in the autumn of 1935 where it was displayed fitted with a Lanova petrol/diesel engine. This was replaced by a standard Dennis O-type oil engine before its delivery to West Yorkshire however. The other new buses making their first appearance were 40 Bristol JO5Gs which arrived between December 1935 and July 1936, although none entered service until 1 January. The 18 rebodied Tigers took up their new duties on long distance services and in September it was agreed to fit the 5 1932 Leyland TD2s with Gardner 5LW oil engines in place of their rather thirsty Leyland petrol units. Similarly all Keighley West Yorkshire's petrol engined TD2s were also converted to Gardner 5LW power units between March and May. Neither Keighley or York received any new vehicles during the year although during the final month, York received some Tilling Stevens B10A2s from the West Yorkshire fleet. These, together with some B10A2s which remained with West Yorkshire and some which were later transferred to Keighley had just been fitted with new Bristol 31-seat rear entrance bodies.

With the Minster forming a magnificent backdrop, recently rebodied Tilling Stevens B10A2 Y244, transferred to York West Yorkshire in April 1934 heads for the railway station on local route 16. (G.H.F. Atkins)

One of the main events of the year was the introduction of route numbers on destination displays. Prior to this, although a route numbering system had existed and had been shown in the company's timetable booklets, these numbers had never been

One of three Gardner-engined Dennis Lancet II 34-seat E.C.W.-bodied buses purchased in 1937, 885 like its sisters spent its entire working life on Harrogate town services.

New to Yeadon Transport in 1929, this Leyland TS1 was rebodied with an E.C.O.C. coach body in 1936 and renumbered 557. Continuing to be used as a relief coach in early post-war years, it is seen here in Wellington Street coach station in its final year in service – 1949.

shown on the vehicles themselves. The new system was obviously appreciated by would-be passengers who now found it much easier to recognise their bus at a distance rather than have to wait until it almost reached them.

1937 began with the purchase of a complete row of 18 cottages at Myrtle Square, Harrogate close to the company's central repair workshops. This it was believed would allow future expansion, should this be needed, without the need to seek various properties at that time. By September, the growing fleet housed at Bradford was in urgent need of more space and so an extension was authorised to the Hammerton Street garage with work to commence as soon as possible. After being frought by numerous problems, the new bus station at Vicar Lane was at last completed and much to everyone's relief was brought into use on Sunday 14 November.

During April a new company was formed under the title of Otley Omnibus Stations Ltd. with a share capital of 8,000 £1 shares with the object of building a new bus station in that town. The shares were subscribed by West Yorkshire and Samuel Ledgard of Armley in proportion to their estimated use of this new facility, the company taking 53.39% and Ledgard the remaining 46.61%. A month earlier, West Yorkshire had gained further interests when they took a 27% share in the Blackpool services taken over by Yorkshire Woollen District from Edwin Box & Sons and A. Wallis & Son and a 28½% share in the Blackpool services taken over by Ribble from Wood Bros. (Blackpool) Ltd.

The fleet was further improved by the arrival of no fewer than 65 new buses comprising 45 Bristol JO5Gs; 3 Dennis Lancet IIs; 2 Dennis Aces and 15 lowbridge Bristol K5G double deckers. Added to these were a number of Tilling Stevens B10A2s which had been fitted with new Bristol bodywork. Ordered for delivery during the following year were another 20 Bristol JO5Gs, although these materialised as the more modern L5G-type when they arrived in 1938.

York West Yorkshire gained 4 new highbridge Bristol GO5G-type double deckers with re-styled ECW bodies while Keighley took delivery of 3 Bristol JO5Gs, 1 Dennis Ace and 6 lowbridge Bristol K5Gs. In addition, both Keighley and York received more rebodied Tilling Stevens B10A2s at the start of the year despite the main company having agreed in November 1936 that these should be of the older B9A type. In total, York took 11 of the rebodied B10A2s and Keighley received 9. Finally, in November York replaced their 3 former Corporation Daimler CH6-type double deckers with a trio of former West Yorkshire TD1s of 1930 vintage which received the Gardner engines removed from the Daimlers.

Fleet standardisation was now nearing completion with Bristol, Dennis and Leyland being the predominant makes and almost all of the buses and coaches acquired with the businesses purchased earlier in the decade had been eliminated. Services too had settled down and the basic network had been completed. West Yorkshire were now operating a total of 97 stage carriage services plus 12 express routes and 7 limited stop services whilst Keighley West Yorkshire had 19 services and York West Yorkshire had 13. Other than minor route or timetable changes, this pattern of operations was to remain unchanged until the outbreak of World War II in 1939.

1938 began with the purchase of a secondhand Karrier 6-wheel lorry which was needed for use as a heavy recovery lorry while later, in September a new Austin Seven car was bought to replace the Morris Minor used by the road inspector. This joined the company's small fleet of cars to which a couple of Morris' had been added in April of the previous year. As far as the bus fleet

The last Dennis buses to be bought were a trio delivered in 1938. Lancet IIs with Dennis oil engines, these were usually to be found on local Harrogate routes but occasionally strayed further afield in their early days. This rather poor view shows 888 in Harrogate bus station soon before its withdrawal from service in 1950.

was concerned, new additions comprised the 20 Bristol L5Gs mentioned earlier and 3 Dennis Lancet IIs with Dennis O-type oil engines and ECW 34-seat front entrance bodies. The 3 former Corcoran Bros. AEC Regals which had been stored during the winter after receiving new Mumford coach bodies in September 1937 made their debut in their new form at the beginning of May and were popular with excursion passengers during the hot summer months due to being fitted with fold-back canvas roofs.

One of the ex.Corcoran AEC Regal coaches, 685, is seen here sporting a predominantly cream livery with red roof in 1949, its final year in service. It was rebodied in 1937 by Mumford and until 1949 featured a fold-back canvas roof.
(J.C.W. Halliday)

Orders were placed in March for 10 Bristol K5G double deckers, 35 Bristol L5Gs and 3 Dennis Lancet IIs for delivery during 1939 (although as stated earlier, the Lancets arrived quickly and were placed in service during July and August). The new intake, when it arrived, would allow the withdrawal of 39 of the Tilling Stevens B10A2 single deckers; 4 Leyland Tigers, the 1931 Daimler and 1 Leyland Cub. Later in the year consideration was given to the vehicle requirements for 1940 and it was agreed to order 34 Bristol single deck buses and 6 Bristol 6-cyl. Gardner engined luxury coaches which would allow the withdrawal of 30 T.S. Motors B49A7s; 10 Tilling Stevens B10A2s and 6 Leyland TS4s.

One of the 1937 ECW-bodied Bristol J05Gs, 105 in its original livery is seen here on the rural service from York to Thirsk in 1938.

1937 Bristol K5G 358 with lowbridge E.C.W. bodywork passes through Headingley on its way to Leeds from Otley in 1939. Ten years later this bus was given a further lease of life when it, along with its sisters, was fitted with new bodywork.

Harrogate's new bus station opened on Friday 1 July, although it was used only by out-of-town services, the local routes continuing to use their stands in Victoria Avenue, Raglan Street and Station Parade. Six months later, the company negotiated the purchase of a 1528 sq.yd. site at Northway, Scarborough where they proposed to build a new bus station and garage. The deal with Scarborough Corporation, the owners of this land was completed in January 1939 and moving quickly, contracts were signed with H. & J. Taylor Ltd. of London in May for the building of these new premises.

West Yorkshire's main fleet 1939 Bristol K5Gs were luxuriously fitted with coach-type seats for use on the Bradford – Keighley service, for which they also were fitted with side destination boards. 392 was pictured here when new.
(E.C.W.)

Both York and Keighley received new buses during 1938, the former taking 11 Bristol K5Gs with stylish highbridge ECW bodywork, the latter being content with 6 lowbridge K5Gs. The arrival of Keighley's new double deckers enabled the last of their open staircased TD1s to be withdrawn and one of these was immediately taken into West Yorkshire's Harrogate workshops for conversion into a tree cutter – the centre section of its roof being removed. Another former Keighley bus, a Tilling B10A2 was also removed from service for conversion into a towing lorry, a fate which was also bestowed upon a York B10A2 and two vehicles of the same type from the West Yorkshire fleet. Upon completion, these replaced the last of the old Karrier tow lorries which themselves had been converted from buses in 1928. One inter-fleet transfer took place on 22 December when one of Keighley's 20-seat Dennis Ace buses was sold to the main company.

At the start of 1938 the company were operating from 14 depots at Bradford, Leeds, Harrogate, Keighley, York, Ilkley, Skipton, Malton, Grassington, Easingwold, Boston Spa, Wetherby, Pateley Bridge and Yeadon and also shared East Yorkshire's Vine Street garage in Scarborough. The Keighley and York garages housed both main fleet and joint-undertaking vehicles whilst the Boston Spa premises were vacated during the early part of the year.

Uncertainty surrounded 1939, with the threat of war looming and viewing this seriously, the company began to erect air raid shelters at certain of their premises during June. Still hoping that peace would be preserved, plans were submitted for the construction of a new bus station in Knaresborough, work on

After the war, 392 gained the new standard Tilling red livery with two cream bands and was transferred to Harrogate depot. Pictured here in Harrogate bus station in 1949, it was withdrawn later that year to be rebodied with new Roe lowbridge coachwork.
(J.C.W. Halliday)

During the immediate pre-war years West Yorkshire amassed a fleet of 95 E.C.W.-bodied Bristol L5G 32-seat buses which featured the company's own traditional styling. One of the 1939 examples, 159 awaits its Knaresborough-bound passengers in Harrogate bus station in 1952.

Below: Resting in Knaresborough bus station in the early 'fifties, York West Yorkshre Bristol K5G Y702 retained its bible destination indicator until its withdrawal for rebodying in 1954.

which commenced in April. Completed in an unbelievably short time, this new terminal point opened during the late summer, at almost the same time as work was commencing on a new bus station at Townfield Gate, Keighley.

The flow of new vehicles continued unabated and making their debut on 1 January were 10 lowbridge ECW-bodied Bristol K5Gs. Although externally being very similar in design to those delivered in 1937, internally they featured Alhambrial ceilings to their lower decks and had luxurious blue moquette covered coach-type seats for 48 passengers – 24 on each deck. All were put to work on the prestigious Keighley to Bradford service in an attempt to attract traffic away from Bradford Corporation's ancient trams on the section between Crossflats and Bradford. Following in February and March were 35 Bristol L5Gs with West Yorkshire's standard design of 32-seat front entrance ECW body. Finally, in October/November came the 6 Bristol L6G coaches with superb ECW 30-seat bodies. Arriving too late to work on the London service for which they had been purchased (this route having already been suspended as a consequence of the war) they were used on a multitude of duties including the Blackpool service which was still running at that time.

Still optimistic about the future and believing that the war would not last long, orders were placed for the 1941 vehicle replacement programme when a further 6 Bristol L6G coaches, 9 Bristol K5G double deckers and 24 Bristol L5G saloons were called for. It was intended that these would replace 21 Leyland Tigers, the 13 Albion PMA28s and the 5 1932 Leyland TD2s. Two additional cars were bought – an Austin in June to replace the Wolseley and a two year-old Daimler private hire car in August as a replacement for the car of this same make which had previously been used for this purpose.

Taking a brief rest in Rougier Street, York enroute to Whitby is 641, one of the ECW-bodied Bristol L6G coaches purchased in 1939. A year after this photograph was taken, 642 was rebuilt and fitted with a post-war type Bristol radiator.

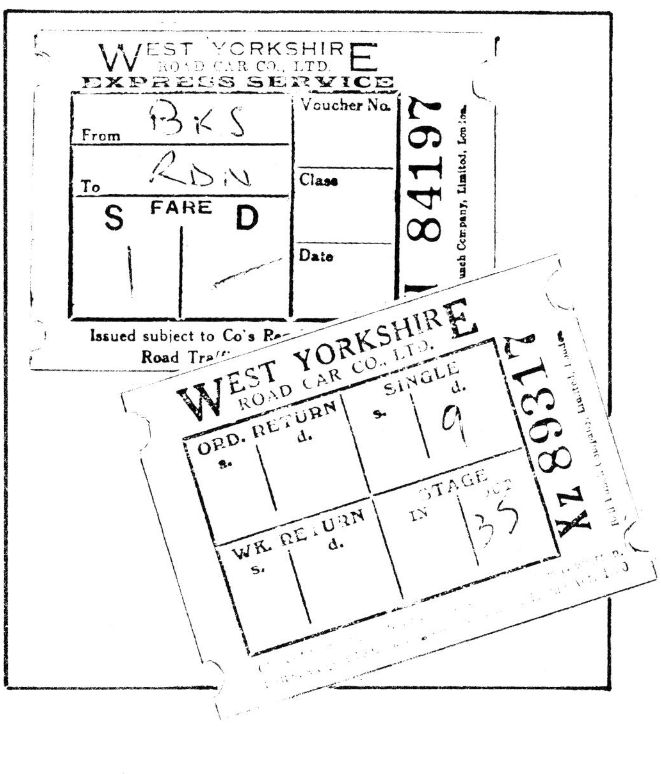

THE DISRUPTIONS OF WAR

War was declared on 3 September and immediately caused a number of services to be withdrawn, truncated or reduced in frequency. Amongst the first casualties was the London service although other long distance routes to the Yorkshire and Lancashire coasts continued to operate for a while longer. Reductions in services allowed an unusually large number of vehicles to be taken out of service and, following Government instructions, the vast majority of these were placed in store rather than sold so as to provide a reserve fleet should this ever be needed. The first withdrawals had already taken place when on 31 August 11 of the T.S. Motors B49A7s had been delicenced. This was the tip of the iceberg however for at the end of the first month of war (30 September) a massive 73 buses and coaches were removed from service. These consisted of 10 Dennis Lancet Is; 25 Leyland Tigers; 28 T.S. Motors B49A7s; 1 Tilling B10A2 and all 9 of the AEC Regals. These were joined on 31 October by a further Lancet I and on the last day of the year by 26 more Lancet Is and another 5 Tigers.

The York and Keighley fleets were also reduced by the withdrawal between September and December of a number of their vehicles. At York service cuts took their toll on 9 Tilling Stevens B10A2 single deckers and 8 of the TD1s were also taken out of service upon the arrival of their replacements, the new Bristol K5Gs. Keighley only lost 4 of their operational fleet, these all being Tilling B10A2s.

When 1940 began, few effects of the war had been felt by the population in general, and believing it to be a phony encounter, things began to become more relaxed. On 21 March West Yorkshire reinstated some of the services curtailed during the previous September and 10 single deckers were brought out of store and returned to service. 45 of the Bristol L5G single deckers (44 for West Yorkshire, 1 for Keighley) ordered earlier arrived between March and May and were built to full peacetime specification. Not being immediately required for service, they were placed in store in various of the company's depots until 1941 when they were licenced for use.

Within the company's area were numerous military installations, munition factories and ordnance depots and all of these required transport mornings and evenings for their employees. This placed a heavy burden on the company's resources which, due to staff shortages, petrol rationing and the many other aspects of war, were becoming stretched to the limit. A wide range of special workers services was set up and in order to maintain these it was necessary to contract some of the operations out to neighbouring operators, including municipalities and independent companies. The need for additional double deckers became of paramount importance and as a consequence all the York West Yorkshire time-expired open staircase Titans were given a new lease of life by being returned to service during the summer and allocated to West Yorkshire garages at Leeds, Bradford, Keighley and Ilkley. Still under-strength for their increased double deck requirements, West Yorkshire hired 10 Leyland TD5s with Park Royal lowbridge bodywork from East Kent. Numbered AJG11-20, the first of these arrived on 26 August and all were in service at the company's Bradford depot by 4 September. Although they retained their original owner's livery throughout their stay, it is believed that some, if not all, gained West Yorkshire fleet names.

Bristol L5G 195 although delivered in 1940 did not enter service until the following year. Its ECW body was built to West Yorkshire's standard pre-war styling and featured the then traditional bible destination indicator.

Prior to the arrival of these double deckers, the company had lost 15 of their single deck fleet when, on 3 July, the Military Authorities requisitioned 12 Leyland Tigers and 3 T.S. Motors B49A7s. These were to be used for the movement of troops in various parts of the country and few remained in their home territory with their new temporary owners.

The new bus station at Townfield Gate, Keighley which had been under construction for some considerable time was eventually opened on 8 September, thus relieving the congestion in the surrounding streets where buses had previously terminated. As the new premises were not large enough to accommodate all the Keighley services however, the new bus station was used basically for the out-of-town routes and local services continued to collect their passengers in the main thoroughfares of the town.

The first real effects of war were felt on the night of 31 August when an enemy bomb fell on the company's depot at Hammerton Street, Bradford, causing a great deal of damage to

Starting its life in 1934 as a 20-seat E.C.O.C.-bodied Dennis Ace bus (606), this vehicle was converted into a depot van in 1941 and continued in this role at Leeds until its final withdrawal in 1952.

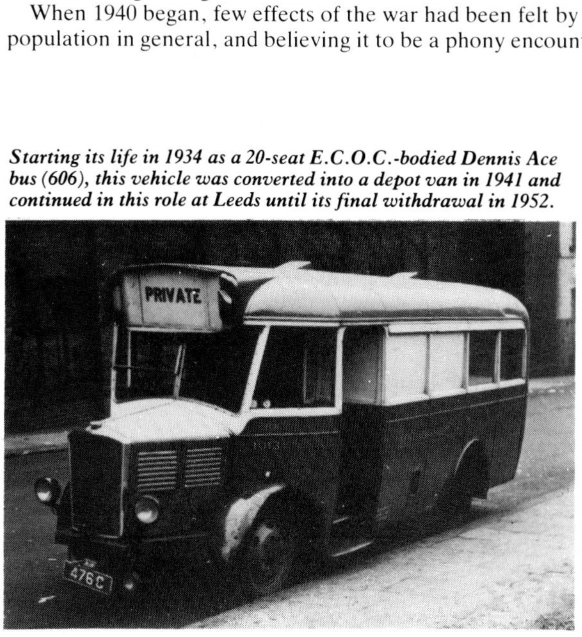

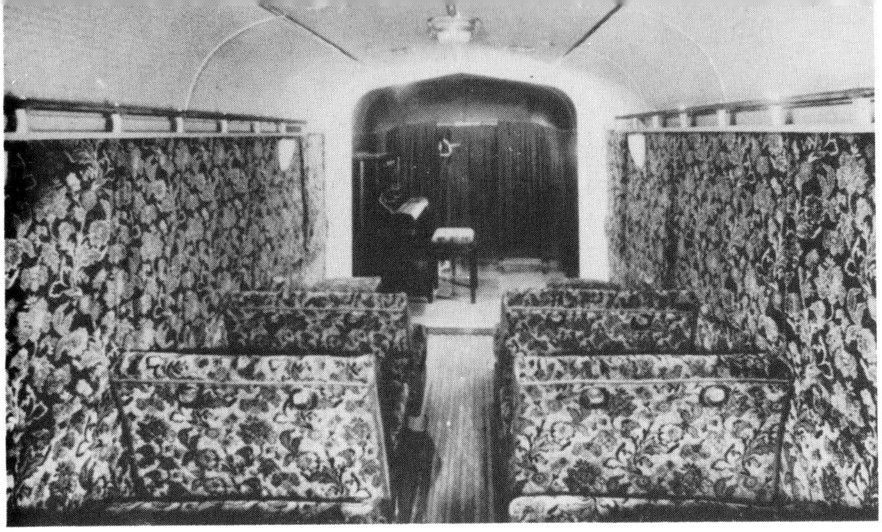

An interior view of 546 after its conversion to a mobile theatre in 1940 for use by ENSA, its rear emergency exit was hidden by the curtains at the back of the stage area alongside the piano.

439 pictured in the early war years still retained its pre-war livery but had gained a grey roof, white wing edges and headlight masks when it was photographed in 1942 in Hawkesworth Estate, Leeds during a diversion of the 32 service to Yeadon.

York West Yorkshire Dennis Lancet Y845 is seen here whilst on loan to London Transport in 1940 operating on country area service 457A from Windsor garage.

the premises and to a number of buses inside. On this same night one of the company's single deckers suffered damage from the explosion of an enemy bomb whilst in service on the outskirts of Knaresborough. Following these incidents, concern grew for the safety of the large number of buses at that time in store and a decision was taken to disperse these to places of greater safety than their depots which, being close to town centres, were vulnerable to future air attacks. After a hurried search, premises were found in rural areas such as Denholme, Cullingworth, Cottingley and Pateley Bridge – these being old mills etc – and were rented on a month by month basis. The new Bristol L5Gs which had not yet entered service were given priority, but as more space was available than was required for these, they were joined by a number of Dennis Lancets and Aces, some Leyland Tigers and even a few elderly Tilling Stevens. Additionally, the company's Yeadon garage which had been closed operationally at the start of the war was also used as a surplus vehicle store, mainly for older members of the fleet.

Following the devastating enemy air attacks on the capital, London Transport sent out a plea for operators throughout Britain to loan them surplus buses in order that they may maintain their essential services. Answering this call, West Yorkshire despatched 17 of their Dennis Lancet Is on 27 October. Upon arrival in London, they were allocated to London Transport's country area around Windsor and Slough where they worked alongside other borrowed buses. Two of York-West Yorkshire's Lancet Is were also loaned to London at this same time.

West Yorkshire themselves suffered a set-back, if only small when one of their 1937 Bristol K5G double deckers – 349 – was destroyed by fire whilst in service on 12 October. Fortunately the chassis was not damaged beyond repair and after being rebuilt at Myrtle Road, it was despatched to Eastern Coach Works where a new body was fitted during the late spring of 1941. This was surprisingly built to ECW's pre-war design and was almost identical to the original body fitted.

One vehicle which served in an unusual role throughout the war years was Leyland TS4 546 which was converted by the body shop at Harrogate into a mobile theatre for E.N.S.A. With its interior completely refitted – complete with a piano, stage and curtained windows it toured military establishments throughout the north to provide much-needed entertainment to the armed forces until 1945.

Despite the war having an effect on raw materials of all kinds, work continued on the construction of the company's new garage and bus station at Northway, Scarborough and this opened on

One of the Hoyal-bodied AEC Regents hired from Halifax Corporation during the war years is seen here in more pleasant pre-war days. Note the peculiarly-humped roof and open rear staircase.

With its roof painted grey and its fleet name painted out, Dennis Lancet I 824 stands forlornly in Belfast in 1942 whilst on loan to the Northern Ireland Road Transport Board. This bus never returned to West Yorkshire, passing direct from Belfast to Caledonian, Dumfries for further hire and later purchase by this Scottish operator.

Saturday 1 March 1941. By this time however, the long distance East Coast services had been withdrawn again and thus the allocation of the new garage was one solitary bus, needed for local operations on the Malton road.

As the need for additional buses at Leeds and Bradford escalated due to the increased demand by the special workers services to the A.V. Roe factory at Yeadon and the R.O.F. at Thorp Arch, the 6 York West Yorkshire Tilling Stevens B9As were sent to Leeds depot on 15 January to provide the required extra capacity. Their stay was short however with 1 being transferred to Wetherby on 8 February and 2 to Bradford on 3 March, and all except one were withdrawn on 30 April and placed in store (the remaining example lasting until 30 June). To compensate, York received the 4 Keighley West Yorkshire Tilling B9As on 15 January, although these too ran their final journeys on 30 April.

The first day of 1941 saw the entry into service of 10 of the new Bristol L5Gs which had remained in store since their delivery almost a year earlier. 9 were placed in the West Yorkshire fleet whilst the other was allocated to the Keighley joint company. Before making their debut, their livery had been altered to incorporate a grey roof – a feature that had been applied to all the company's vehicles during the autumn of 1940 so as to make them less easily seen from the air. The usual blackout features of white mudguard tips and edges, white step edges and a thin white band at the bottom of their lower panels were of course included, as were headlight masks and reduced interior lighting.

On 24 April, a total of 12 Dennis Lancet Is left the company to cross the water to Northern Ireland on loan to the Northern Ireland Road Transport Board who were in dire need of additional buses to transport workers involved in essential war work. To compensate for this loss, the remaining 25 new Bristol L5Gs were placed in service from 1 May, the additional 13 enabling a similar number of petrol-engined single deckers to be placed in store due to petrol being more difficult to obtain than diesel fuel. The Lancets which had assisted London Transport during their hours of need began to return home during July and by the end of August all were back with the company. Many of them went directly into storage whilst those which returned to West Yorkshire service proudly carried plaques on their cabs proclaiming 'London 1940-41' as recognition of London Transport's appreciation.

In addition to the buses loaned out to other operators, West Yorkshire also provided a number of vehicles, complete with drivers, for use by the Armed Forces at bases throughout Yorkshire. This meant that the drivers had to stay in Army or R.A.F. camps for several days at a time whilst on these duties and on several occasions they came under attack from enemy aircraft. One such incident on 9 April at Linton Aerodrome led to Dennis Lancet 814 suffering extensive damage and as a result, the chassis, after rebuilding, had to be despatched to Eastern Coach Works at their temporary wartime home at Irthlingborough where a new body was fitted. This was constructed from parts in stock to its orginal pre-war design during July.

In order to replace the old Bean depot vans, four of the company's Dennis Ace buses were taken out of service during the summer, and were rebuilt into vans for use at various depots for the carriage of spares etc. They took up their new duties at the start of September.

Still being optimistic in their belief that the war would not last much longer, the company placed orders for their 1942 vehicle replacement programme despite the fact that their previous orders were still unfulfilled. These called for 24 Bristol double deckers of the K5G-type and 15 single deckers of the Bristol L5G-type which it was intended would replace 43 Dennis Lancet Is in due course. Similarly York-West Yorkshire ordered 5 highbridge Bristol K5Gs for the replacement of 7 Tilling B10A2s whilst Keighley specified 6 lowbridge K5Gs as replacements for 10 Tilling B10A2s.

The need for the greater movement of passengers led the Government to introduce the Emergency Powers Defence (Road Vehicles Standing Passengers) Order, 1941 during the autumn. Under this act, single deck buses fitted with perimeter seating were allowed to carry up to 30 standing passengers, depending on the service on which they were operated. As a result, and to give conductors guidance on the number of standees they were expected to allow, their Fare Tables were coded so that each service shown carried a CSD code. In general terms, this allowed 24 standing passengers on normal services, 30 on works services and 12 on more rural routes or operations of a special nature. In compliance with this new emergency order, the company converted a number of their Bristol J and L-type buses to perimeter seating, thus reducing the seating capacity from 32/34 to 30 but enabling the number of passengers to be doubled with the standees.

Before the year ended, a further 2 Leyland Tiger TS3s were requisitioned by the Military Authorities when in November 520/9 were taken by the Air Ministry.

1942 proved to be an eventful year in many different ways and started with the loss of 390, one of the 1939 Bristol K5G double deckers which was extensively damaged by fire on 1 January while in service. Its chassis was subsequently rebodied by ECW in August and although externally this was to full pre-war design,

Keighley West Yorkshire Brush-bodied Bristol GO5G K302 leaves Skipton on route 10 to Keighley in 1944 in full wartime khaki livery, complete with headlight masks, white wing edges and route stencil box below its canopy.

internally it showed the restraint placed on manufacturers by the lack of materials resulting in a spartan appearance with single-skin panels throughout. Eastern Coach Works were also called upon by the company to assist them with heavy bodywork maintenance and during 1941/2 several buses were despatched to Irthlingborough for major body overhauls including three of the L6G coaches of 1939 vintage, a couple of L5G buses and several G05Gs.

Still being desparately short of buses, the Northern Ireland Road Transport Board asked West Yorkshire if they were able to loan more of their stored fleet, and in answer to this plea, the company despatched a further 20 Dennis Lancet Is to Belfast on 15 March. Although having a surplus of single deckers, West Yorkshire themselves were still in need of higher-capacity vehicles with which to maintain their war factory services, and in particular, those serving the A.V. Roe works at Yeadon. In an attempt to ease this situation, 3 elderly AEC Regent double deckers were hired from Halifax Corporation on 19 March and immediately put to work from Bradford depot. In their grey livery with brown relief bands, these buses became regulars on the 55 service from Bradford to Yeadon as well as on certain of the Avro duties, although being of highbridge configuration, they could not be used on routes from Bradford via Greengates due to the low railway bridge at Eccleshill (despite Bradford Corporation successfully operating highbridge buses under this obstruction on their services).

Until the late spring of 1942, West Yorkshire had retained its pre-war red and cream livery – albeit with the addition of grey roofs – and had made no concession to any of the drab wartime colour schemes employed by other operators. In May however, at the instruction of the Ministry of War Transport, all buses used on war factory services had to be painted in camouflage colours and as a consequence, West Yorkshire began to transform a number of their single and double deckers into a dull khaki-grey livery from this date. The process was slow however and it was not until 1944 that all the vehicles concerned were thus treated.

In the quest to save fuel, tyres and other essential materials, the company's services again came under review and many more suffered reduced frequencies, particularly in the evenings and at weekends. Mileage was saved by the altering of several terminal points and thus reducing the length of certain routes, even if only by short distances. Amongst these were the 30/31 services from Bradford and Keighley which were altered to terminate at Leeds Wellington Street bus station rather than operate across the city to Vicar Lane and the 32 Leeds – Yeadon and 55 Bradford – Yeadon routes which had their Yeadon termini changed from Town Hall Square and the White Swan respectively to Albert Square, a saving of about ¼ mile on each. Posters began to appear on buses exhorting people to 'Save paper to win the war' and to use public transport by such slogans as 'Tyres are rare, save yours' whilst internally a wide range of bills posted in vehicles warned passengers to 'Be like Dad, keep Mum' and not employ casual conversation which may pass on secrets useful to the enemy or enquired 'If their journey was really necessary'.

More strange buses arrived on 2 August when 8 old-fashioned looking AEC Regents from London Transport suddenly appeared. These were at first allocated (in full London livery) to Leeds and Harrogate depots, but being somewhat slow when compared with the company's own Bristols, they proved unsatisfactory and on 1 January 1943 were all transferred to York West Yorkshire in exchange for 8 of that undertaking's Highbridge Bristol G05Gs. Following the arrival of the London STs, the 10 East Kent Leyland Titans returned to their rightful owner on 19 August, their place at Bradford being filled by a general reallocation of the company's Bristol double deckers. Joining the exodus were 26 of the T.S. Motors B49A7s which were sold during August to Bristol Tramways & Carriage Co. Ltd. for further service after having been stored by West Yorkshire since their withdrawal from service in 1939. Additionally, one of the B49As requisitioned by the Ministry of War Transport in 1940 was re-purchased in October and this too was sold to Bristol to join its brethren.

The Dennis Lancet Is began to return from Northern Ireland at the end of September and at the end of the year only 5 remained in Belfast. 6 of these buses, rather than being returned to West Yorkshire were despatched direct from Northern Ireland to Caledonian Motor Services of Dumfries to whom they were hired from 9 November. Of these, two returned home to West Yorkshire on 20 December, the other four remaining with Caledonian to whom they were eventually sold on 1 October 1943.

The only new addition to the fleet during the year was a

Leeds Vicar Lane bus station in 1942 is the setting for borrowed London Transport AEC Regent ST249 seen leaving for Harrogate on service 36. Also evident is an East Yorkshire Leyland Tiger and a G. F. Tate Leyland Lion LT5.

Khaki-liveried 557, a rebodied Leyland TS1 ex. Yeadon Transport, stands outside Grove Park depot, Harrogate in 1943 after being converted to operate with a gas-producer trailer.

A wartime view of Bristol G05G 338 in khaki-grey livery with white edges to its front wings and lower panels. Several dented panels are visible as a reminder of the lack of body maintenance during the war years.

secondhand 1937 Wolseley staff car which was purchased in August. The Lanchester car which had been used as a spare since 1939 was converted into a small pick-up truck during September, taking up its new role in the service vehicle fleet at the start of the following month.

At the request of the Ministry of War Transport West Yorkshire arranged to acquire and operate 40 gas producer trailers, the first of which made their debut in October. In view of it being easier to convert petrol-engined vehicles to run on producer gas than it was to modify diesel engines, 19 Leyland Tigers were taken out of store for this purpose. All operating from Harrogate depot, they soon became a familiar sight towing their smoking and often smelly trailers. Due to their limited operational range and sluggish performance, they were confined to local town services. 928, one of the Gardner diesel-engined Bristol J05G single deckers was also converted to haul a gas-producer trailer whilst sister bus 927 was used experimentally with a built-in gas producing unit.

By now the special workers services to munition, aircraft and armourment factories were at their peak, requiring large numbers of buses each morning and evening. As co-ordinators for many of these operations, West Yorkshire, not having sufficient vehicles of their own, had to contract out to other operators in order to meet their requirements. Some of the vehicles concerned were hired for specific journeys each day on a regular contract basis whilst others were hired for longer daily periods. Among the latter were a number of Sheffield United Tours coaches which, with their drivers, were based at West Yorkshire depots for use on the contracts from Harrogate to Thorp Arch Ordnance Factory during 1942 and from 18 December from Harrogate and York to Allerton Park. Similarly, S.U.T's subsidiary company United Motor Services Ltd. of Sheffield were contracted during 1942 to provide two coaches for the Bradford to Thorp Arch contract which terminated on 23 January 1943. Another Sheffield-based operator, Hibberds Tours also provided two coaches for West Yorkshire duties in 1942, these being released in February 1943.

Perhaps the most important development of 1942 however was the separating of Tilling and British Electric Traction interests by the winding up of the Tilling-British Automobile Traction holding company. In this division West Yorkshire and its associated companies passed to the Tilling Group in which it remained until nationalisation in 1948.

An unusual purchase made in January 1943 was that of a secondhand 30hp Ford V8 car of 1938 vintage. This it was intended was to be operated on producer gas, although it is not known whether it pulled a trailer or had its production unit built into its boot. Meanwhile, on 5 January eight of the Leyland TS3s requisitioned in 1940 were re-purchased from the Military Authorities and were duly collected from Army depots at Leicester and Sheffield. A further TS3 was re-purchased in February and similarly the solitary TS4 taken over by the Army was also returned to company stock (from an Army base at Plymouth) in June. The remaining 2 Leyland Tigers and 2 T.S. Motors B49A7s never returned to West Yorkshire and apart from one of the B49A7s which continued to serve with the Armed Services until 1945, the others are thought to have been destroyed by enemy action. The remaining 5 Lancets returned from Northern Ireland during the early part of the year, the last arriving back in Harrogate on 23 January.

Another surprise acquisition during the year was made in July when an eight year-old Dennis Ace single decker was purchased from John T. Hey (Silver Star), Skipton. Upon arrival at Harrogate, this little bus was immediately dismantled to provide a source of spares for the Aces still in service with West Yorkshire.

The flow of Bristol G05G double deckers to Eastern Coach Works continued spasmodically throughout 1943/4 for heavy body overhaul and the repainting of vehicles into khaki-grey livery proceeded steadily during this period. The war dragged on and left in its wake, a rapidly declining fleet due to shortages of materials and manpower. Buses whose life span would in normal circumstances have ended several years earlier continued to give yeoman service and it was not known when these would now be able to be replaced.

After an uneventful start, 1944 saw the company purchase a plot of land known as the Feast Field at Pateley Bridge in June. This it was thought would provide a site for a new depot at some future date when building work was allowed to re-commence. With similar thoughts in mind, land was also purchased from the LNE Railway adjacent to the station at Malton in November, although like Pateley, this was not developed for many years.

As West Yorkshire's daily vehicle requirements subsided slightly, it was found possible to release 4 of the London Transport AEC double deckers which were returned to their rightful owner between 18 August and 1 September. Replacing them at York were a pair of York's highbridge Bristol G05Gs and 2 open-staircased Leyland TD1s which had been on loan to West Yorkshire since earlier in the war.

Harrogate bus station in the early summer of 1949 shows two soon to be withdrawn vehicles. 1939 Bristol KG5 388 was shortly to be fitted with new Roe lowbridge bodywork whilst Lanchester 1007, converted from a staff car into a pick-up truck early in the war was almost at the end of its life.

All the gas producer buses were withdrawn on 31 October following an easing in fuel rationing, and whilst no-one was sorry to see these go, they had served a useful role and allowed services to continue to operate during one of the most difficult periods of the hostilities. After spending a few months in store, the 40 trailers were eventually broken up for scrap during the early months of 1945.

On the following day (1 November), the first new bus to be delivered since 1940 made its debut at Bradford. A Bristol K-type with AEC 6-cyl. oil engine, it was fitted with an austere lowbridge body built by Strachan to Ministry of Supply specification. Of extremely spartan appearance and internal finish, it was equipped with a single-piece roller blind destination indicator at the front instead of West Yorkshire's more customary metal 'bible' type of fitting and thus was the first new double decker so treated since the TD1s in 1930. Seven days later, another double decker was placed in service, this time at Leeds depot. This was a K5G of 1943 vintage which was fitted with ECW's prototype post war highbridge body. Owned by Western National, JTA 271 spent much of 1944 touring the various Tilling Group companies and was hired by West Yorkshire from 7 to 24 November. Another stranger in the fleet at around this same time was a United Automobile Services lowbridge Bristol K5G which was loaned to Keighley depot in exchange for a Keighley West Yorkshire K-type which earlier in the year had been fitted with an experimental Bristol 6-cylinder engine.

The only new buses delivered during the war to Ministry of Supply specification were five Strachan-bodied Bristol K6As which arrived in 1944/5. All were rebodied with pre-war bodies removed from K5Gs in 1949/50 and prior to this, 708 is seen leaving Chester Street bus station, Bradford early in 1949.

With the Allied Forces now starting to make some headway towards ending the long years of war, some of the earlier restrictions began to be slightly relaxed and during the late spring of 1945 the company was able to re-introduce Sunday services on some routes which had been devoid of these since the early 'forties. Lighting restrictions were eased and, to many, it seemed as if the end of the torment was at last in sight. Looking towards the future, the company purchased 4136 sq. yds of freehold land from Odeon Cinema Holdings Ltd. at Woodhouse Lane/ Merrion Street, Leeds during May and at this same time bought a dwelling house in West End Avenue, Harrogate.

Between March and June, four more Strachan-bodied Bristol K6As entered service at Bradford and as the vehicle requirement to the wartime factories was reduced, so the withdrawal of a large number of time-worn buses commenced. Several of the York-West Yorkshire Leyland TD1s used by Bradford, Leeds and Ilkley depots since 1940 were either withdrawn or returned to York; the remaining York highbridge Bristol G05Gs went home; the last Tilling Stevens single deckers in the fleet (at Keighley) made their final journeys and a number of Dennis Lancet Is, now surplus to requirements were placed in store. Continuing the policy of soliciting outside help for heavy body overhauls, a large number of Bristol J05Gs, Leyland TD2s, York G05Gs and Dennis Lancet Is were despatched to ECW or a number of independent coachbuilders (Woodhall Nicholson of Halifax; Croft of Glasgow; Plaxtons; Burlingham; Maudslays of Leeds; Chas. Roberts of Horbury; Edmunds of Middlesbrough and Cawoods of Leeds) during the year. A start was made on the repainting of the khaki-grey buses back to red and cream, although the application was now changed to reduce the area of the lighter shade. On single deckers cream continued to be applied to the window surrounds but the roof was red whilst on double deckers an all-over red livery was introduced, relieved only by cream bands below the upper deck windows and at upper deck floor level. For matters of obvious economy, the pre-war ornate lining out was discontinued, although the red and cream areas were separated by black beadings. Several experimental livery applications were applied during 1945 before that mentioned above became the new standard.

From October 1945, all the bodies overhauled by ECW were fitted with roller blind destination indicators at the front. The vehicles concerned were some of the Leyland TD2s and a number of Bristol J05Gs and this marked a slow end to the 'bible'

930 was one of only five 1936 Bristol J05Gs to receive roller blind destination equipment upon rebuilding in 1946. This view taken on 8 July 1950 shows it operating a free shopper's service to Busby's store in Bradford.

Below: Several of the 1932 Leyland TD2s gained roller blind destination indicators in place of their original bible equipment when they were rebuilt by E.C.W. in 1945. 440, the last surviving TD2 is seen in Keighley bus station during its final months of service in 1949.
(J.C.W. Halliday)

destination boards which had been a feature of the company since 1930. As will be seen later however, the faithful 'bible' was to survive for several more years and it was not until 1958 before it was finally eliminated. In addition to receiving heavy body overhauls, a large number of the G05Gs and J05Gs had their chassis rebuilt by the company during the period 1945-7, more often than not using new chassis sides supplied by Bristol. These buses could now almost be regarded as new vehicles and this undoubtedly extended their lives longer than would have been had they remained unrehabilitated.

Following the lifting of the restriction by the Ministry of War Transport which forbade operators to sell or scrap vehicles during the period since 1939 (without first gaining permission to do so), West Yorkshire began to dispose of a number of their older vehicles, some of which had spent many years in store. Amongst these were several Leyland Tigers and some Tilling Stevens as well as the gas-producer Ford V8 car and a Daimler limousine. Further vehicles to depart were 10 of the Albion PMA28s which had last run in 1939/41. These were requisitioned by the Ministry of War Transport on 12 May for use in Germany by the French Commission.

The last four London ST-type double deckers were returned to London in September and December and on the last day of the year 2 of the Halifax Corporation AEC double deckers also returned home. The war was now at an end, and West Yorkshire were no doubt thankful that they had escaped the worst effects of the hostilities, being out of the range of the enemy's pilotless weapons and being largely unpunished by more conventional air attacks.

A RETURN TO PEACE

A new year – and a new era – dawned, and plans were laid for a return to full peacetime standards in terms of both the fleet and the company's operations. The service network began to recover from the previous cutbacks and frequencies were restored and routes reinstated in order to meet the new demands from a relieved population seeking to pick up the threads of normal life. The process was naturally slow as rationing was still in force and there was still a general shortage of materials and equipment, but the gradual return to peacetime standards was at last under way.

Further inroads were made into the stock of obsolete vehicles with the sale of the last of the Tilling Stevens and Albion single deckers, the old Bedford lorry – for which a replacement in the form of a new Bedford had arrived in August – and a Daimler staff car. The delivery of new vehicles was still slow however, and only 9 double deckers and 2 single deckers were received during the year, of which 6 were for the Keighley and York fleets (3 double deckers each). The first of these to arrive were the 3 Keighley Bristol K5Gs which entered service on 25 March. Fitted with ECW's new standard post-war lowbridge bodies, these buses had that manufacturer's early-style rectangular ventilators to their side windows and were fitted with Tilling-type roller blind two-piece destination screens at both front and rear and also on the nearside above the open rear platform. Surprisingly their livery incorporated only one cream band at upper deck floor level and it was not until 1951 that a second cream band beneath the upper deck windows was added by the company. For West Yorkshire, 3 identical buses arrived on 29 March, entering service on the same day and these, like the Keighley examples were fitted with Bristol's new low PV2-type radiator. The York trio did not make their debut until the beginning of July and differed from the Keighley and main fleet buses in having highbridge bodywork – and two cream bands. The two new single deckers did not materialise until 1 September. Utilising Bristol L5G-type chassis they had ECW's new post-war style of body with a rear entrance protected by a sliding door and seating for 35 passengers. Having the same style of ventilator windows as their double deck counterparts, they had two-piece roller blind destination indicators at both front and rear and also featured a single piece screen above the rear nearside wheel arch. As a result of the arrival of the new double deckers, the last of the hired vehicles – an AEC Regent – was returned to its owner, Halifax Corporation on 31 March. Also withdrawn were the last of York's open staircase Leyland TD1s, the final example surviving until the last day of the year.

Realising that the orders placed in 1939 and 1941 which were still unfulfilled no longer took into account the company's needs, these were superceded early in July by orders for 5 Bristol double deckers with Strachan bodies (already delivered in 1944/5); 5 Bristol double deckers and 20 Bristol single deckers for 1946 and 10 Bristol double deck, 10 Bristol single deck, 4 Bedford coaches and 4 Bedford buses for delivery in 1947. For Keighley, new orders were similarly placed for 6 Bristol double deckers for 1946 and 6 Bristol double deck and 2 Bedford buses for 1947 whilst at York the requirement was for 5 Bristol double deckers for 1946 and 10 Bristol single deckers for 1947. Some of these had of course already been delivered, although the remainder of those specified for 1946 did not arrive until the following year.

During the early part of 1946 the company had suffered a set back when Leeds Corporation placed a compulsory purchase order on the land acquired during the previous year at

The first post-war buses purchased by West Yorkshire were a trio of lowbridge Bristol K5Gs which arrived in 1946. 714 seen here in Templar Street, Leeds in 1950 still carried only one cream band despite having had its side destination indicator removed.* *(G. H. F. Atkins)

The first post-war single decker was this E.C.W.-bodied Bristol L5G which arrived in 1946. Seen here in Otley bus station some thirteen years later, it still retained its original body with square-top sliding ventilators above its windows.
(J.S. Cockshott]

This late 1945 view of Bristol GO5G 315 at Calverley shows it in one of the experimental liveries of that time with cream upper deck window surrounds and between-decks band. This was to be shortlived however and 315 reverted to standard Tilling red & cream in 1946.

Woodhouse Lane/Merrion Street. Still reeling from this decision, West Yorkshire were further incensed when their plans for a new garage on the land they owned alongside Malton railway station were rejected by the local authorities.

Following discussions with Tadcaster Tower Brewery Ltd. who were the tenants of the Craven Arms at Skipton, the company agreed to sell these premises to them and to purchase them back at an agreed sum as and when a transfer of licence to other premises was obtained. The completion of this sale took place on 31 May 1947.

Templar Street, Leeds is also the setting for this view of 1947 Bristol K5G 715 which unlike the previous year's K-types was delivered with two cream bands. As can be seen, it retains its side destination screen in this 1948 view.

One of the Bristol L5G single deckers specially built to enable them to pass under the low railway bridges at Leeman Road, York

By the end of 1946 all the company's services had been resumed in full, except that an odd one or two of those for leisure purposes withdrawn in 1939 had not been re-instated, and the sudden demand frequently led to long queues at peak periods even when duplicate buses were used. Concentration had however been on the stage services rather than the express routes and the latter were resumed more slowly.

1947 began with the arrival of more new buses when a trio of Bristol L5Gs were placed in service on New Year's Day. These were identical to those of the previous year as were two of the five L5Gs which made their debut on 25 March. The remaining three had an improved style of bodywork in which the side ventilators were more neatly incorporated into the windows. More followed between May and July when a further ten took up their duties. On the double deck front, only two new arrivals came during the year, both being Bristol K5Gs which entered service in May. These too had the neater style of ECW body and, unlike their predecessors were delivered complete with two cream bands. Keighley received three more lowbridge K5Gs of which two featured the new design of sliding ventilators, the other having the earlier style of body. All three however had two cream bands and the excessive number of destination screens.

The first post-war coach delivered to the company was 646, a Bedford OB-Duple 26-seater which made its debut in 1947. It is seen here in Northway bus station, Scarborough with one of its sisters on excursion duties. Both coaches are wearing their original cream & maroon livery.
(G. H. F. Atkins)

One of a pair of ex.War Department Ford Canada trucks purchased in 1946 for use as towing lorries reclines in the sunshine outside Bradford depot in the early 'fifties.

York took delivery of 5 new buses, a pair of highbridge K5Gs with new-style windows which made their appearance in March and 3 single deck L5Gs in September/October. The latter were unusual in having a single piece destination screen at both front and rear, the front box being built flat to the roof to enable operation beneath the low railway bridges in Leeman Road, York.

The first new post-war coaches materialised in the form of two of the four Bedfords ordered in 1946. Of the famous OB-type with Duple Vista 26-seat coachwork, the first of these made its debut on 1 July, its sister not arriving until October, and a month later came the first of the Beadle-bodied Bedford OB buses, although this did not take up its duties until the first day of 1948.

For the ancillary fleet, two ex.War Department Canadian Ford lorries were purchased on 1 January 1947 for use as towing vehicles at Harrogate and Leeds depots and their arrival allowed the withdrawal of the Karrier recovery lorry and one of the converted Tilling Stevens buses. To provide another depot van, one of the 1934 Dennis Aces was withdrawn from service and converted at the company's own workshops, taking up its new duties at Bradford depot in November whilst a new Austin 8hp staff car was bought in January.

A start was made on the disposal of the fleet of Dennis Lancet Is and during the year a total of 15 were sold, plus 3 from the York fleet and a further 3 were dismantled for spares. Some of these buses had remained in store since their withdrawal in 1939 whilst others had only received major body and chassis overhauls during the previous year. Also sold were several of the petrol-engined Leyland Tigers.

New vehicles seemed to be uppermost in the company's mind, and during 1947 no fewer than three major orders were placed. For the main company fleet, 8 lowbridge Bristol double deckers and 30 Bristol single deckers were specified for delivery in 1948; 18 Bristol lowbridge deckers, 20 Bristol single deckers and 6 Bristol single deck coaches were ordered for 1949 delivery and 6 Bristol lowbridge double deckers, 25 Bristol single deckers and a further 6 Bristol coaches for arrival in 1950. During May, the previous year's order calling for 4 Bedford buses was reduced to 2. Similarly, orders for Keighley and York spread over this period called for 14 lowbridge Bristols and 16 highbridge Bristols respectively. Even the car fleet was taken into account in November when it was agreed to purchase 7 new Austin A40 cars for use by inspectors for delivery as soon as possible. In March 1948 however, it was thought that the programme of new vehicles for 1948 and 1949 may be appreciably reduced to help the export market and it was therefore decided to place an order for 15 new double deck bodies for delivery in 1948 and 10 in 1949 to be fitted to the 1937 and 1939 Bristol K-type chassis respectively.

1948 saw the delivery of no fewer than 57 new vehicles for the combined fleet with West Yorkshire taking 2 Bedford OB Duple-bodied coaches, 2 Bedford OB-Beadle bodied 30-seat buses, 17 Bristol-engined K-type double deckers, 3 L5G saloons and 10 Bristol L6B 31-seat dual purpose vehicles. Keighley

Classified as dual-purpose vehicles, the 10 Bristol L6Bs delivered in 1948 were fitted with coach-type seats for 31 passengers. One of these vehicles, 656, is seen in Wellington Street coach station, Leeds at the start of its limited stop journey to Newcastle in 1950.

736, one of the lowbridge Bristol K6Bs of 1948 vintage prepares to leave Otley bus station on the 34 service to Leeds in April 1953. (J.S. Cockshot)

One of a pair of Beadle-bodied Bedford OBs bought by Keighley West Yorkshire in 1948, K617 still retained its full destination display when caught by the camera in 1953. In common with the other Bedfords in the combined fleet, it later had its destination aperture reduced to show a single line.

York West Yorkshire Y758, a Bristol K6B turns out of Northway bus station, Scarborough with its destination blinds showing white blanks. Note it still retains its side destination screen in this 1950 scene.

West Yorkshire Bristol JO5G 996 shows the way in which spare metal 'bible' destination boards were carried during long duties on a variety of routes. The destination shown within the destination holder was carried on an 'H' slipboard which did not display any intermediate points. (J. C. W. Halliday)

Two views of 251 and EG1 show the former at Hawes in July 1951 carrying a destination board below its front canopy whilst the latter, pictured at Richmond in July 1955 had by that time had a centre divider fitted to its rear window, thus making it unique amongst West Yorkshire's 7ft.6in. wide L-type single deckers. (J.C.W. Halliday)

gained a pair of Beadle-bodied Bedford OBs and 7 lowbridge Bristol K6Bs while York received the remaining 7 of their special-bodied L5G single deckers and 7 highbridge K6B deckers. Amongst these were the first Bristol-engined buses in the fleet other than the experimentally fitted 1937 K-type.

UNDER STATE OWNERSHIP

In May 1948, the position of the negotiations which were in progress for the amalgamation by the British Transport Commission of the omnibus undertakings in the Tilling Group were outlined to the company and it was only five months later, in September when the announcement was made that the nationalisation had been completed.

One of a trio of standard E.C.W.-bodied Bristol L5G buses delivered in 1948, SG132 stands on the forecourt of Harrogate's Grove Park depot in the late 'fifties.

During the late summer, withdrawal of the 1937 Bristol K5Gs began, and after receiving a complete chassis overhaul – including in many cases the fitting of new chassis sides – and being given more modern PV2-style radiators, they were despatched in batches to ECW where they were to receive new lowbridge bodies. In addition to the 15 West Yorkshire K5Gs, 6 of Keighley's pre-war buses of this type were also thus treated. Of the main fleet buses, 2 were returned fitted with non-standard destination displays which incorporated a separate route number.

Comparatively few new vehicles were added to the fleet in 1949 as a result of the rebodying programme and for the main company, only 6 Bristol K6Bs and 6 dual purpose L5Gs arrived along with an integrally-constructed Beadle-bodied Morris Commercial 35-seat single decker. This had a rear entrance and full-width cab and was powered by a Saurer diesel engine. For the Keighley fleet were 10 lowbridge K6Bs whereas York only gained half that number, all of course with highbridge bodywork. These new additions saw the withdrawal of the last remaining Dennis Lancet Is which had struggled out their final days on Harrogate town services, the last of the Leyland Tiger single deckers and Titan TD2 double deckers, and the remaining Dennis Aces. In order to speed up the overhaul procedure, a body float was created for the Bristol J05Gs using the Roe body from the prototype Dennis Lancet II and a similar float was set up for the York highbridge GO5Gs with the body removed from Y316 which was to be converted to a towing lorry. These floats resulted in a number of body exchanges being made, this continuing through 1949 to 1950.

In preparation for the second phase of the K5G rebodying programme, a start was made on the withdrawal from service of the 1939 batch and the 1938 Keighley buses, plus a solitary 1937 example from Keighley which had escaped the earlier programme. The best 5 of the old bodies removed were transferred to the chassis of the wartime Ks whose Strachan bodies were then scrapped. In similar fashion to that undertaken earlier, all the pre-war Ks were given thorough chassis overhauls and were fitted with PV2-type radiators before being despatched to the coachbuilders to receive their new bodies. On this

All West Yorkshire's 1937 K5Gs were given new E.C.W. lowbridge bodies in 1949, two of which were fitted with non-standard experimental destination displays. One of this pair, 353 is seen in 1953 on Harrogate local service 12 before its destination screen was replaced by one of standard layout.

The oddman out amongst the York-West Yorkshire Bristol K6Bs was Y763 which was built to 4-bay specification. This 1952 view of Y763 shows its side destination indicator which has been painted over and the draught deflectors which were originally fitted to the sliding ventilator windows.
(West Yorkshire)

938 ended its life carrying the Roe body removed from prototype Dennis Lancet II 882. As can be seen, this differed in many ways from the E.C.O.C. bodies fitted to West Yorkshire's JO5Gs of the 1935/6 period.

Above: 709, one of the wartime Bristol K6As is seen here after being fitted with the pre-war ECW body from a 1939 Bristol K5G.

A surprise purchase in 1949/50 was a pair of Beadle-bodied Morris Commercial 35-seat buses. Both spent the whole of their lives working from Harrogate depot and 619 is seen here in the town's bus station.

occasion they were sent to Chas. H. Roe of Leeds however, due to ECW being stretched to the limit at that time, and when they began to return in April 1950, they were immediately distinguishable by the totally different design of their new lowbridge bodies.

Finding themselves short of coaches for the summer season of 1949, West Yorkshire hired 4 Duple-bodied 29-seat Bedford OB coaches from Cumberland from June until the end of August. This, as will be seen later became a regular occurrence during the summers of the next few years.

A number of services were altered during 1949, albeit in a minor way and the Harrogate to Boroughbridge routes were extended onwards to Aldborough. New services to make their debut were a local route from Ilkley to Hebers Ghyll, a Tuesday and Saturday only service from Harrogate to Stonehouse Inn and a Malton town service form Hawthorne Avenue to Beverley Road. Additionally, during the spring of 1950 the Leeds to Harrogate and Harrogate to Ripon routes were linked together to provide a through service from Leeds to Ripon, although United continued only to operate jointly from Ripon to Harrogate.

1950 opened with the entry into service of the year's first new buses and during the months that followed, a variety of new types were taken into stock. For Keighley were 3 lowbridge K6B double deckers whilst for York were 6 highbridge K6Bs. The main fleet received 14 L5G saloons, 15 lowbridge K6Bs, another Beadle-Morris Commercial, their first 30ft. long single deckers in the form of 4 LL5Gs, the first proper post-war coaches – 6 L6Bs with full-fronted bodywork, 6 27ft. long KS6B double deckers and, more surprisingly, the second prototype Bristol Lodekka. This was a revolutionary design in which normal highbridge type bodywork with centre upper deck gangway was fitted to a specially lowered Bristol chassis to give an overall height of only 13ft. 4in. Entering service on 23 March with Bristol Tramways and Carriage Co., it passed to Brighton Hove & District on 2 April, staying with them until 9 June when it finally reached Harrogate. Working mainly on the Harrogate – Leeds service, it departed on 6 January 1951 to undertake a tour

One of the 1939 Bristol K5Gs fitted with a post-war PV2-type radiator and rebodied by Roe in 1950, 394 stands at the rear entrance of Hammerton Street depot, Bradford in 1953.

of various Tilling Group companies who operated it in service until 16 June when it was returned to its makers for renovation. This being completed, it was then placed on display at the Festival of Britain Exhibition on London's South Bank from 21 August until the end of September, returning to West Yorkshire on 1 October 1951.

Right: West Yorkshire received the second prototype Bristol Lodekka in 1950. Numbered 822 it spent much of its early life on the prestigeous Harrogate to Leeds service on which it is pictured here at Harrogate bus station in 1953.

Below: West Yorkshire only bought six lowbridge Bristol KS6Bs, all of which made their debut in 1950. 811 rests in Harrogate bus station in 1953 at the start of its long journey to Skipton on the 76 service.

During the mean time, disaster struck in February 1950 when Bristol GO5G 336 overturned on Harewood Bank whilst operating the Harrogate – Leeds service. Surprisingly it was not withdrawn as a result of this accident (despite a start being made during this year on the withdrawal of the GO5G and JO5G types) but was fitted with the body removed from a Keighley GO5G and was returned to service on 1 May. As in the previous year, 4 Duple-bodied Bedford OB coaches were hired from Cumberland from June, this time staying until the end of September. 1950 also witnessed the demise of the remaining Dennis Lancet IIs.

On the management side, J. C. Dean left the company on 31 May to take up a similar appointment with Bristol Tramways, Mr. H. N. Tuff replacing him as general manager on the following day.

In Keighley, the first major service change since the introduction of the Hainworth route during the previous summer came on 20 December when a second service was started between Keighley and Riddlesden via a different route. Due to it crossing the Leeds & Liverpool canal, it had to be operated by single deckers as did the original Riddlesden service, but conversely, on 1 January 1951, the 21 to Spring Bank was converted from single to double deck operation. Later in that year, on 17 June, the Keighley town services underwent major revision and many of the old cross-town routes were re-linked to different termini.

More GO5Gs and JO5Gs were withdrawn and to replace them came 13 more Bristol LL5G single deckers with 7ft. 6in. wide bodywork, and the first 8ft. wide buses to join the fleet. These comprised 6 Bristol LWL6B 39-seat saloons, 12 LWL6B full-fronted luxury coaches, 14 KSW6B lowbridge double deckers and 8 LL5G 39-seaters with 8ft. wide bodywork outrigged on 7ft. 6in. wide chassis. For York, who still preferred 7ft. 6in. wide buses due to the narrow city streets they had to traverse, 4 highbridge KS6Bs arrived and Keighley received 6 LL5G saloons. All the double deckers had open rear platforms although the main fleet KSWs were all fitted retrospectively with platform doors during 1954. In an attempt to improve passenger comfort, some of these new buses were fitted with saloon heaters

The first proper full-sized coaches to be received since 1939 made their debut in 1950 in the form of six full-fronted Bristol L6Bs. Wearing its original cream livery with maroon wings, 660 stands in Harrogate bus station in 1952.

The first four Bristol KSW6Bs (new in 1951) originally carried their front registration plates on their radiators rather than below the windscreen. Numerically the first, 806 at Bradford bus station can be seen in its orginal form.

York West Yorkshire YDG60, a pre-war Bristol K5G was fitted with a post-war PV2-type radiator and new E.C.W. highbridge body in 1951.

and during the year a start was made in adding this luxury to all the main fleet post-war bodied buses which had not been so equipped when new. In order to assist drivers to easily identify the 8ft. wide buses, these were all fitted with white steering wheels and it was not until several years later that these began to be interchanged with the otherwise standard black type.

Having now completed the main fleet K5G rebodying programme, a start was made in giving similar treatment to the 11 K5Gs delivered to York in 1938. These all had their chassis overhauled and fitted with PV2-type radiators before being despatched to ECW for fitting with new highbridge bodies early

Left: 1937 Bristol J05G 987 after being converted into a mobile information bureau and renumbered 1018.

Below: Due to the city's narrow streets, York West Yorkshire continued to purchase 7ft.6in. wide buses in 1952. YDB87, a Bristol KS6B carried highbridge bodywork in common with the remainder of the York fleet.

Rebuilt into a double deck coach in 1951, Bristol K6B 751 is seen here before its entry into service in its new form. It was later relegated to normal bus duties after being re-seated to conventional 55-seat layout.

Above: Twelve 8ft. wide Bristol LWL6B coaches were bought in 1951 and fitted with E.C.W.'s re-styled 35-seat coachwork. 674 on a private hire duty in 1952 shows its original cream livery.

Resting in Templar Street, Leeds alongside Vicar Lane bus station in 1952 is KSW6B 831. Although delivered with an open rear platform, it had doors fitted in 1954.

in the year, and all but two were back in service in their new form in May/June, the remaining two following in October. By this time a start had been made on the removal of the side destination indicators from all the double deckers so fitted, although internally the destination box itself was left in situ.

The company's ticketing system was updated on 28 March when the first of 100 Setright machines were brought into use at Yeadon depot where they replaced the Bellgraphic

Keighley West Yorkshire's first new post-war single deckers were Bristol LL5G 39-seaters delivered in 1951. KSGL19 (originally K420) carries one of the short-lived (and difficult to read) fleet number plates on its cab side.

Automaticket machines. So successful were the new Setrights that a further 230 machines were purchased before the end of the year. The Ultimate tickets introduced in 1949 for use on local services continued to be used on such however until June 1960 after which the Setright reigned supreme.

Perhaps one of the most striking reminders of 1951 was the conversion of one of the main fleet Bristol K6Bs into a double deck coach. Entering central works in January, 751 was completely stripped internally and was then equipped with 21 luxurious coach seats to its upper deck (in rows of three, with arm rests between each seat) and 20 to its lower deck. Luggage space was provided behind the rear upper deck seat, over the rear wheel arches in the lower saloon and beneath the staircase. Heaters were added to each deck and rear platform doors were fitted. Mechanically, the autovac was replaced by a CAV pump and a 5-speed gear box was added in place of the original 4-speed unit. Painted in a predominantly cream livery with red relief flashes, it re-entered service in its new form in May on the Keighley – Scarborough service.

Whilst work was being carried out on 751, the chassis of 934, a 1936 Bristol JO5G was also in the company's central workshops undergoing experimental work. This had been lengthened forward of the front axle and its Gardner 5LW engine was then re-mounted on this extension. By chance, during February 1952 after all the mechanical work had been completed, 965, one of the 1937 JO5Gs sustained front end damage in an accident and as a result was withdrawn from service. The remainder of its body

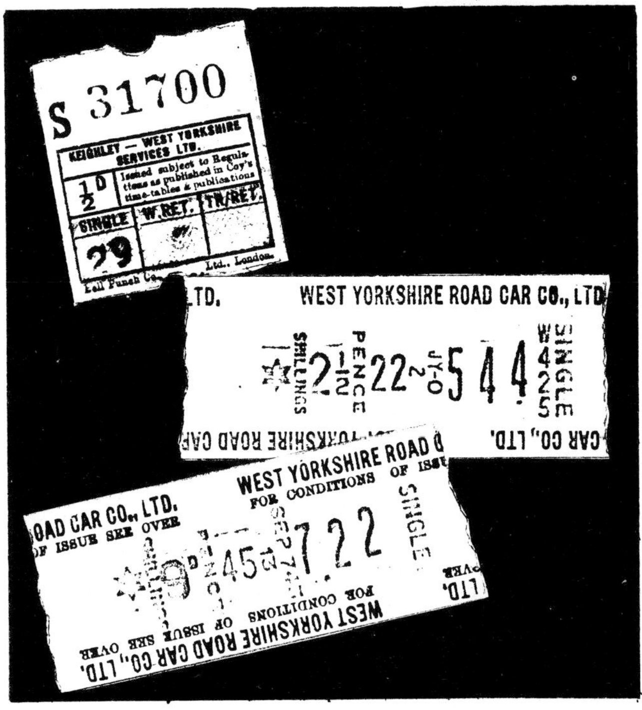

The rebuilt chassis of Bristol JO5G, lengthened to 30ft., was fitted with the modified body of 965 whose registration number it carried. Pictured here on an enthusiast tour in 1955, it was withdrawn from service two years later.

Above: While West Yorkshire 830 was on loan to United for evaluation of its experimental staggerd seating. United loaned the company one of their 1947 Bristol K6Bs, JHN462. It is seen in Harrogate bus station in December 1952 with a paper sticker in its destination screen (and another in the lower deck front bulkhead window) to signify its operation on the 36 service to Leeds. About to overtake it is 1939 Bristol L5G 137.

being undamaged, it provided the basis for a new body for 934 and in due course it was fitted with a new full-width front end, the entrance being alongside the driver and forward of the front axle. The whole of the body was heightened by the extension of its lower panels, and as a 44-seater it entered service in its new guise (with the fleet and registration number of 965) at Leeds depot on 1 August 1952.

One of the 1953 Bristol KSW6Gs, 857 is seen here when new.

During the first month of 1952 a new service was started from Shipley to West Royd Crescent to serve a new housing development and a few months later another new service was commenced from Bradford to another new housing estate at Owlet Hall. Following these developments came the news that Baildon Council had agreed to allow double deck operation on the various services into the town from Bradford for a trial one month period (the routes previously being confined to single deckers), and after seeing this to be a success and causing no problems, double decking became the norm. During the summer, on 2 July, a new service was inaugurated from Harrogate to Grassington via Pateley Bridge, this proving popular with those wishing to visit the countryside, especially at weekends and holiday times.

The first underfloor engined vehicles in the fleet were five Bristol LS6G coaches which were purchased in 1952 for use on the London service. One of these, CUG4 is seen here at Yeadon Airport operating the special coach service to Bradford during the late 1950s.

A pair of SGW-type 8ft. wide-bodied Bristol LL5Gs with 7ft.6in wide chassis illustrate the appearance of these outrigged buses as they rest at Benton Pcrk School, Rawdon.

During 1952/3 a large number of former West Yorkshire Bristol J05G and G05Gs were sold overseas. This view shows the bodies of 312, K904, K903 and 333 near Ostend docks, Belgium after their chassis had progressed to Holland. After being equipped as lorries, they were then exported yet again to India and Pakistan.

Wartime Bristol K6A DG41 which had its AEC engine replaced by a Gardner 5LW unit in 1947 was given the 1937 E.C.W. body from K5G K366 in 1950 and lost its bible destination indicator in favour of a roller blind type two years later.

Above: The last front-engined, half-cab single deckers purchased were Bristol LWL6Bs which arrived in 1952. One of these, SBW29 rests between duties in Templar Street, Leeds.

The pre-war Bristol L6G coaches were all given a facelift in 1952 when their front ends were rebuilt by West Yorkshire and they were fitted with PV2-type low radiators. 640 seen in its 'new' form carries the all-cream livery used on these coaches until 1953.

The property in Victoria Avenue, Harrogate known as the Belvedere which the company had bought in 1934 became the subject of a compulsory purchase order by the County Council who wished to construct a new College of Art on the site. Having little option, the company sold this area to the Council later in the year.

New vehicles to arrive were 20 Bristol LWL6B saloons, 18 lowbridge KSW6Bs, 1 KSW6G and 5 LS6G underfloor-engined coaches for the London service. For York came a further 6 highbridge KS6Bs. The new coaches were the first underfloor-engined vehicles to join the fleet and were painted in a cream livery with black window surrounds. Of the KSW6Bs, one – 851 – was taken directly into central works before entry into service for conversion to a double deck coach. The work involved was far greater than that on 751 during the previous year and when the new coach finally emerged, it was hard to imagine that it had ever been a standard bus. Super luxurious, it incorporated many interesting features and had seating for 51 passengers of which 27 were carried on the upper deck. All its side windows were of the non-opening type and it was fitted with an electrically driven air conditioning system. Perspex panels were inserted into its roof and a different internal colour scheme was employed on each deck. Luggage space was provided by racks above the nearside lower deck seats and an enclosed luggage space beneath the stairs was accessible from the rear. Platform doors were of course fitted and externally it was finished in a striking black livery,

The first of a large number of Bristol LS5G dual purpose vehicles, EUG1 is seen soon after its entry into service in 1953 wearing almost bus-like red & cream livery.

The striking black livery with its abundance of chrome-plated trim can clearly be seen in this view of double deck coronation-year coach 851 as it stands outside Scarborough depot whilst working the express service to Bradford.
(G.H.F. Atkins)

Vehicles were hired from a variety of neighbouring operators to assist with the movement of the large crowds attending the Air Display at Yeadon each year during the fifties. Included amongst the buses used in May 1959 was Todmorden J.O.C. Leyland PD2 no.17 seen here at Albert Square, Yeadon.

One of the withdrawn Bristol J05Gs, 107, was converted into a mobile display as part of the company's Coronation celebrations. In this form it toured West Yorkshire's various operating areas in company with 851, the luxurious double deck coach and CUG4, one of the LS6G coaches seen in the background.

lined in white and incorporating chrome-plated flashes and wing contours. In its new form it made its debut on 21 May 1953 and was used by Bradford depot on the Scarborough service.

Meanwhile, a number of the unrebodied York pre-war K5Gs and the 5 pre-war bodied main fleet wartime Ks had their bible destination indicators replaced by roller blind equipment and four of the 1952 Bristol LWL6B saloons together with a 1948 K6B had their Bristol engines replaced by Gardner 5LW units. In August, KSW6B 830 was experimentally fitted with staggered seating to its upper deck in place of the more conventional bench-type seats associated with lowbridge buses and after being tested in service, it was loaned to United in December for evaluation by that company. In exchange, United loaned the company one of its 1947 Bristol K6Bs with standard ECW lowbridge bodywork. Further loans to the company came in the form of six Duple-bodied Bedford OB coaches from Crosville and 4 of this same type from Lincolnshire for the month of June.

Wishing to update their 1939 Bristol L6G coaches which were now looking somewhat old fashioned with their high shield-type radiators, the company rebuilt the cab area of their bodies with deeper windscreens and fitted them with PV2-type radiators during 1952. After re-seating them with 31 luxurious coach-type seats, they were repainted into an all-cream livery before being returned to service.

For the ancillary fleet, one of York's highbridge GO5Gs was transformed into a mobile paying-in office for use at Rougier Street, York whilst in the previous year a JO5G had been lavishly converted into a mobile information bureau. A further JO5G was converted in 1953 into a mobile Coronation display by the removal of most of its side window pillars and the fitting of a 'moving belt' containing a display of the Coronation procession. This toured the company's area during the summer of 1953 together with the newly converted black double deck coach and one of the new LS6G coaches which was suitably decorated with bunting etc. This trio gained much valuable publicity for the company during their Coronation Year tours around West Yorkshire.

Various experiments were carried out during the year in connection with the then new Cave-Brown-Cave heating system and two of the 1951 LL5G single deckers were fitted with this equipment behind and above their front destination screens.

The usual hiring of Duple-bodied Bedford OB coaches again took place when 4 were received from Lincolnshire on 1 May, returning home on the last day of June. New buses joining the fleet in 1953 were 3 Bristol LS6G coaches, 5 LS5G dual purpose vehicles and the last conventional lowbridge double deckers to be purchased – 2 KSW6B and 9 KSW6G. Also arriving was one of the Bristol pre-production LD6B Lodekkas with ECW 58-seat bodywork. When delivered, it had an open rear platform, 4-speed gearbox and no heaters and was not even given a fleet number. Looking completely different from any other bus in the fleet with its concealed radiator and wide bonnet, it was placed in service at York on 17 May. After only one week in service it was loaned to Cumberland on 27 May, passing to United on 17 June and finally returning to West Yorkshire on 4 July. Moving to Harrogate depot later that month, it was returned to its

West Yorkshire received one of the pre-production Bristol LD6G Lodekkas in 1953. At first not allocated a fleet number, MWR618 is seen here in its original form with open rear platform. It was later returned to ECW to receive platform doors and was numbered DX2.

The second batch of Bristol LS6G coaches had bodywork which eliminated the wrap-round front corner windows. CUG10 seen here was new in 1954.

manufacturers in March 1954 where it was fitted with saloon heaters, rear platform doors and a 5-speed gearbox.

After being confined to single deck vehicles since its inception, the busy 50 route from Bradford to Otley which passed under a low railway bridge at Yeadon was finally converted to double deck operation on 11 May, thus providing Yeadon depot with its first ever permanent double deck operation (although since 1951 deckers had been borrowed for Saturday duties on the 33 service from Rawdon to Leeds). The rural 81 service was cut back from Terrington to Sheriff Hutton on 7 March and on 4 October a new service was introduced from Leeds to Wetherby via Boston Spa, the old route to Boston Spa now being diverted at Clifford and continued to Tadcaster. During the following year, on 24 May, a new service was started amid much publicity from Leeds to Farsley.

The first production Lodekkas arrived in 1954 when 2 LD6G and 9 LD6Bs joined the fleet. These, like all the company's future Lodekkas were already equipped with 5-speed gearboxes and platform doors. More underfloor-engined Bristols also arrived in the form of 7 39-seat LS6G coaches and 13 LS5G 41-seat dual purpose machines. Further Cave-Brown-Cave experiments were carried out using a withdrawn pre-war L5G which had this equipment fitted in the position normally

Above: York's recovery wagon from 1950 to 1964 was Y1005, a former York-West Yorkshire Bristol GO5G double decker (Y316) which was fitted with the cut-down Brush body from Keighley West Yorkshire K302.

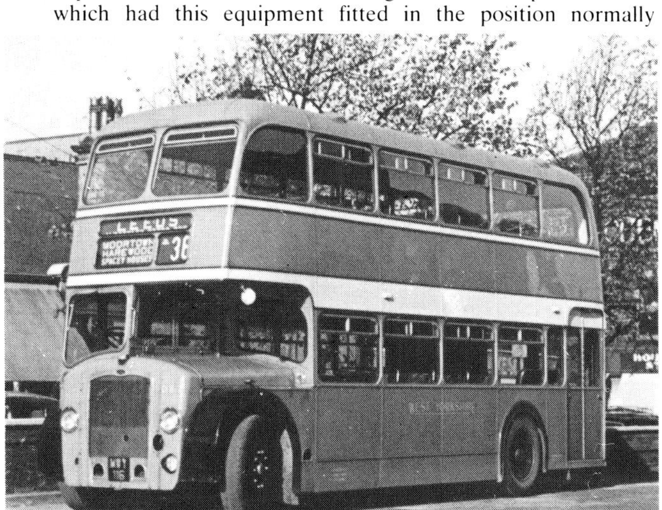

Right: DX7, one of West Yorkshire's first batch of production LD6B Lodekkas was fitted with a full-length radiator grille and three-piece destination screens at front and rear.

A view of Yeadon depot in 1952 showing the double deck garage, an operational Bristol L5G (177), a group of stored withdrawn G05Gs and a withdrawn J05G.

occupied by its bible destination indicator. It never re-entered service however and apart from a few sorties around Harrogate on trade plates, it spent most of its time in the company's central workshops. Following the success of the experiment with staggered upper deck seating, a number of KSWs were so fitted as were, more surprisingly, 5 of Keighley's 1948 K6Bs.

An important change within the company came in April when the entire fleet was renumbered, using type identification letters in addition to more conventional numbers. The first letter signified whether the vehicle was a double decker (D), single decker (S), dual purpose (E) or coach (C). The second letter denoted the engine mark i.e. Bristol (B) or Gardner (G) whilst the third letter denoted 30ft. long (L) or 8ft. wide (W). There were of course some idiosyncrasies such as CUG (Coach underfloor engine Gardner) for LS6Gs and DX for Lodekkas, which one can only presume indicated double decker experimental. Similarly the Bedford OB coaches became CP (coach petrol) and the Bedford buses SP. Keighley and York buses continued to have their numbers prefixed by a K or Y.

An unexpected purchase on 3 October was that of 3 elderly AEC Regent double deckers from Brighton Hove & District. Their chassis dated from 1931/2 whilst their highbridge ECW bodies had been built in 1944 to what could be described as almost post-war design. Although bought by West Yorkshire, these three buses were for loan to the York fleet to cover for the 1939 K5Gs which were to be rebuilt and rebodied during 1955 in batches of three. The AECs duly took up their duties, complete

1940 Bristol L5G 182 was used during 1954/5 for Cave Brown Cave heating experiments following its withdrawal from revenue-earning service. Its new equipment was fitted to the front dome in the position normally occupied by its bible destination indicator and its auto-vac was raised higher up its front bulkhead.

Several of the 1939 Bristol K5G highbridge buses of York West Yorkshire had their bible destinations replaced by roller blind equipment in 1952-4. The last to be so treated was YDG74 in August 1954, just a year before it was withdrawn for rebuilding/rebodying.

Rebuilt from one of the 1939 Bristol K5G chassis and fitted with new E.C.W. highbridge bodywork in 1955, YDG88 was also re-registered to give it the appearance of a brand-new bus.

Bought by West Yorkshire and hired to York West Yorkshire to provide temporary replacements for the 1939 Bristol K5Gs while they were being rebuilt/rebodied were a trio of elderly AEC Regents from Brighton Hove & District. All having been rebodied in 1944, they gave but eleven months service in York before being withdrawn.

Bristol SC4LK 724APU was borrowed from Eastern National in April 1955 for evaluation purposes. Seen here at work on Harrogate local service 17, it looked strange in its green livery in an area dominated by red.

Former dual purpose Bristol LS5G SUG1 which had been reseated and downgraded to bus status in 1957 was experimentally fitted by West Yorkshire with Cave Brown Cave equipment. As this was mounted in the front roof dome, its destination screen had to be moved from its customary position to below the windscreens.
(J.S. Cockshott)

with York fleet names on 1 January and remained in service until 30 November.

Meanwhile, the York K5G chassis were extensively rebuilt using new chassis sides and PV2 radiators before being sent to ECW to receive their new highbridge bodies. Upon their return they were not only renumbered but were also given new registration numbers, thus making them almost brand new vehicles. Genuine new vehicles added to the fleet in 1955 comprised 27 Bristol dual purpose LS5Gs, 5 LS6G coaches and 17 LD6B Lodekkas whilst Keighley received its first Lodekkas with 5 LD6Bs being taken into stock. Further KSWs and K6Bs were fitted with staggered upper deck seating whilst 2 of Keighley's K6Bs were fitted with rear platform doors and saloon heaters for use on the Colne service. The usual hiring of Bedford OB coaches was made again, with 4 Lincolnshire examples being borrowed in June. Numerous other coaches were hired from independent operators on busy summer Saturdays as traffic demanded, and this form of assistance was continued until recent times. The mobile information bureau, Bristol JO5G 1018 spent the first half of the year on loan to London Coastal Coaches who used it as an office in Euston Square, London and then in August it went on loan to United Counties at Northampton where it remained until March 1956.

On the operational side, Leeds City Transport surrendered their licences from Leeds to Guiseley and Menston Hospital which were both well outside the city boundary and these were taken up by West Yorkshire on 1 May. This allowed a general reorganisation of services to take place within Aireborough which included the linking of the Leeds to Yeadon and Yeadon to Bradford services to provide through facilities. Wishing to consolidate their position further in this area, the company set up a meeting with Exors. S. Ledgard on 5 July where an exchange of services was suggested. West Yorkshire offered to pass their 27.4% of the total mileage of the joint 34 service from Leeds to Ilkley via Otley together with the whole of their 77 service from Ilkley to Otley to Ledgard in exchange for Ledgard's two services from Otley to Horsforth and their share of the jointly-operated 33 service from Rawdon to Leeds. Finding this suggestion unacceptable, Ledgard refused any such exchange, but still keen to 'clean up' in the Aireborough area, West Yorkshire set up another meeting a year later, on 28 June 1956 when modified proposals were put forward. This simplified the exchange of routes with a suggestion that the company would withdraw from the joint Leeds-Otley-Ilkley route in exchange for the two Horsforth-Otley services presently operated by Ledgard. An additional suggestion made was the separate exchange of West Yorkshire's share in the jointly operated Rawdon-Leeds service for Ledgard's former B. B. Tours route from Bradford to Harrogate via Menston Village. Again Ledgard declined on both counts and it was not until 1967 that West Yorkshire finally gained full control of Aireborough.

Returning to the fleet, a further loan taking place in 1955 was that of an Eastern National Bristol SC4LK 35-seat bus which was used in service in Harrogate from 28 March to 2 April for evaluation. Although the company found this bus to be satisfactory they never purchased any of this type.

1956 opened with the acquisition of the stage service of Bronte Bus Co. of Haworth from Haworth to Stanbury. Taken over on 1 January, no vehicles were acquired and Bronte's other service to Laneshaw Bridge was immediately discontinued. On the same

SUG16, although demoted to stage carriage status in 1959 retained its dual-purpose coach type seats. Two years later, it was futher transformed by losing its dual purpose livery in favour of standard red bus colours.

SUG38, one of the LS5G dual purpose vehicles taken into stock in 1955 is seen in 1959 in Rougier Street, York after arriving on the 43 service from Leeds.

day part of the company's depot at Yeadon was leased to Aireborough U.D.C., this comprising the whole of the six-bay single deck garage which was used by its new tenants as a store for boats from the nearby Tarn. Another portion of the older part of Yeadon depot was leased to the Yeadon Yachting Club for storage purposes at this same time. A further development during January was the opening of a new depot and bus station at Pateley Bridge, the old premises in the station yard being vacated at this time, but as is often the case, the 'official' ceremonial opening did not take place until 29 March, this being carried out by the deputy chairman of Ripon & Pateley Bridge R.D.C. Later, in July, work began on the extensions to Vicar Lane bus station at Leeds, this involving the demolition of everything except the office block and the total redesigning of the whole loading area. The work was completed in less than six months and the new bus station was brought into use on 29 November. Finally, work commenced on the construction of a new bus station and depot at Grassington on 10 December and this was opened during the following summer.

The only new vehicles to enter service during 1956 did so with the main fleet, with 15 dual purpose LS5Gs and 16 LD6B Lodekkas making their debut. In order to extend the lives of some of the 1946/47 L5Gs which were now suffering from the effects of the use of unseasoned timber in their body framework, one of these buses – SG105 – was sent to ECW during the summer for fitting with new all-metal body sides. This was the prototype for other similar vehicles which were to be rebuilt in the company's own body shop and these were duly completed with the use of new body sides supplied in kit form from Lowestoft. One of this same batch – SG103 – was rebuilt more dramatically however, as a 30-seater with its entrance moved from the rear to the front to allow it to be used for one-man-operation. Rather than remove its original rear door, this was locked in position whilst the drivers door was panelled over, thus causing the driver to enter his cab from inside the saloon, part of the front bulkhead having been removed. In its rebuilt form, SG103 re-entered service at Harrogate where it was used mainly on local services, but it was soon transferred to Grassington for use on the Dales routes and here it remained until its final withdrawal in 1962. Various experiments were carried out during the year including the fitting of a supercharged Gardner 5LW engine to one of the LD6G Lodekkas. Another Lodekka – DX14 – met with a serious accident in Leeds on 22 January when it left the road and plunged into a beck. So extensive was the damage that it had to be returned first to Bristol and then to ECW for extensive rebuilding.

Also returned to ECW were the first of the company's dual purpose LS5Gs (EUG1-8) which were reseated to stage carriage specification with accommodation for 45 passengers.

Finally, on 16 December as a result of the fuel restrictions due to the Suez crisis, numerous service cuts had to be made. Particularly effected were operations after 6.30pm each day and all day Sundays when frequencies were cut dramatically. Happily this situation did not last too long and normal operations were able to be resumed on 7 April 1957.

During 1957 a variety of experimental work was carried out in the company's own workshops including the fitting of two double deckers – DB6 and DG34 with exhaust brakes, the fitting of EUG52 with coil springs instead of the more conventional leaf type and trying out glassfibre front nearside wings on several

Tragedy struck on 22 January 1956 when almost-new Lodekka DX14 plunged into a beck in Leeds whilst operating the 36 service to Harrogate. After extensive rebuilding at Bristol and E.C.W, it returned to service six months later.

vehicles. Additionally, Lodekka DX59 was given 'Loadmeter' equipment which visually recorded the number of seated passengers being carried at any given time. In addition, the equipment marked a graph which could then be used by the traffic department for analysis purposes. Following the success of this experiment, several other vehicles of the DX and SUG-types were similarly equipped, but on this occasion without the visual passenger counter.

The extra air vents cut in the front wings of DX2-43 had not proved as effective as had been hoped and as a result these vehicles were gradually fitted with the shorter type of front wing as used on later Lodekkas. Two more of the 1947 L5Gs (SG107 & 109) were fitted with new body sides whilst in the autumn one of the two withdrawn Morris Commercials was taken into the body shop for conversion into a depot van, emerging in its new guise in October. Earlier in the year, the sole surviving Duple-bodied Bedford OB coach, CP1, was completely rebuilt for continued use on the York City Tour, a duty it had performed since 1954. Given perspex cant and roof panels with lift-up type ventilators, air conditioning, sliding ventilators to its side windows, a one-piece rear window, single destination screen and modern external mouldings, its appearance was extremely

1947 Bristol L5G SG103 was converted to front entrance configuration in 1956 for one-man-operation. Its rear door, although left in situ was permanently locked and its conventional sliding window ventilators were replaced by air ducts above the windows. It is seen here soon after re-entering service in its new form on a Harrogate town service.

CP1, one of the four Duple-bodied Bedford OB coaches was extensively rebuilt in 1957 for use on the York City Tour, a duty on which it continued to be employed until 1968. Happily this little coach has survived in preservation.

DX59 was the first Lodekka delivered to the company fitted with Cave Brown Cave heating equipment. This can be seen at each side of the front destination screen and this LD6B new in 1959 was also the first of its type to have fixed glazing to its upper deck front bulkhead windows.

updated whilst internally it was trimmed with formica lining panels and was fitted with a public address system.

An innovation in July was the introduction of fleet number plates made from pressed aluminium. Fitted to the cab side and rear panels, they were intended to replace the old type of transfer but on finding them difficult to read at anything more than a few feet away, they were soon discontinued. Although only 52 vehicles were ever thus equipped, plates had been purchased for the whole of the fleet and rather than waste them, they were thereafter used in the cab and inside the saloon in a position close to the entrance door.

The only additions to the fleet were 12 Lodekkas of the LD6B-type and a solitary dual-purpose single decker. This was a pre-production Bristol MW5G with ECW 41-seat body which was placed in service on 1 November. Of the Lodekkas, 4 had spent some months in store at Pateley Bridge depot before entering service in April whilst the final 5 to be delivered differed from the previous type by having Cave-Brown-Cave heating systems and fixed glazing to their upper deck front bulkhead windows. Among the vehicles withdrawn from service during the year was 965, the experimental lengthened JO5G.

For the ancillary fleet, a former War Department AEC Matador was bought, its body being replaced by a new one built in the company's own body shop at Harrogate. Equipped for heavy recovery duties, it eventually took up its new duties in February 1958 when it replaced Leyland TD2 1004 at Harrogate depot.

Only two Bedford OBs were hired from Lincolnshire during this year, both arriving on 1 June and returning home at the end of the same month. Meanwhile the down grading programme concerning the EUG dual purpose vehicles to 45-seat stage carriage status continued with EUG6-8 being thus treated by ECW in January/February and EUG9-12 being despatched to Lowestoft at the end of the year, returning early in 1958. Upon being re-seated their fleet numbers were changed from EUG to SUG.

The opening of the new bus stands in Shipley Market Place on 1 June resulted in all but one of the services passing through this town being diverted to serve this part of the new shopping centre whilst on the following day the 66 circular route was withdrawn and replaced by a new service from Bradford Canal Road End to Shipley. A month later, on 7 July, the Skipton-Harrogate and Harrogate-Tadcaster services were joined together to provide through facilities and on 30 September a new town service in Skipton from Greatwood Avenue to Horse Close Estate replaced the former route which operated only from the town's bus station to the Horse Close housing development.

During February, plans were outlined for the demolition of the company's premises at Wetherby and for the erection on that site of a new bus station and garage. It was however some time before these plans came to fruition as will be seen later. Towards the end of the year a small plot of land owned by the company at White Cross, Guiseley was sold to Aireborough Urban District Council.

Perhaps one of the more unusual innovations of 1957 was the free pushchair service which was launched by the company on 5 December in Harrogate. By showing a ticket proving that they

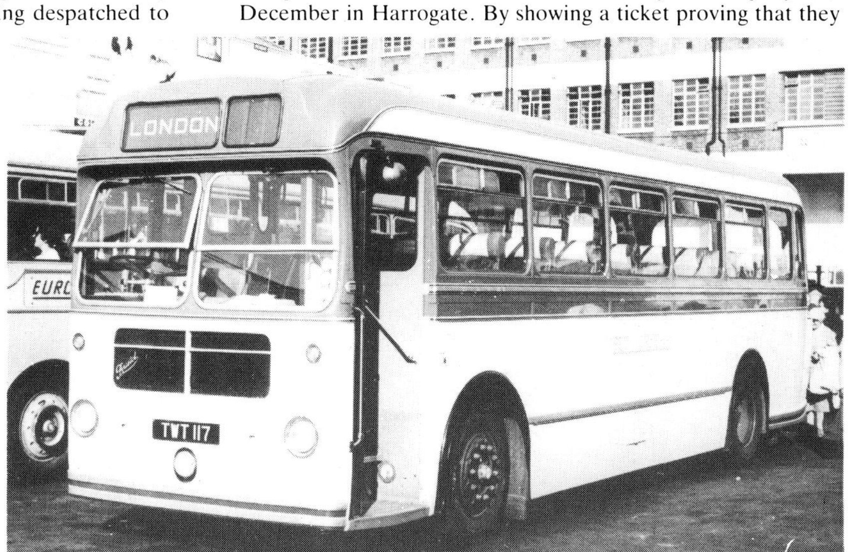

EUG64, a 1958 dual-purpose Bristol LS5G is seen during the following summer in Victoria Coach Station, London where it has just arrived on the long service from Leeds.

had travelled into town by bus, mothers (or of course fathers) were able to borrow a pushchair from the enquiry office in the bus station. As well as no charge being made, there was not even a deposit to be paid and this new service was available each day Monday to Friday between 9.0am and 5.0pm.

The one feature which marred 1957 was the 'Provincial' bus strike which effected bus operators throughout the country except for London. Beginning on 19 July it was to last for 10 days during which time West Yorkshire's entire platform staff withdrew its labour and buses were at a complete standstill. It eventually ended on 29 July, but by that time irrepairable damage had been done and many passengers, having found alternative methods of travel, never returned to the buses.

After a comparatively quiet start, 1958 witnessed more than the usual crop of service changes amongst which was a new limited stop service between Bradford John Street and Keighley bus station. Numbered X67, the buses used on this route were fitted with special destination blinds with a blue background and from its inception on 21 April this new, fast facility gained popular support. An application for a new service from Rutland Close, Harrogate to Vicar Lane, Leeds was surprisingly withdrawn whilst on 30 November the Harrogate-Boroughbridge and Knaresborough local services underwent complete revision.

The fleet was updated by the addition of 5 LD6B Lodekkas, 3 MW6G coaches and 8 LS5G express single deckers whilst Keighley and York each received 3 Lodekkas. These replaced the 5 wartime Bristol double deckers, the first of Keighley's post-war K5Gs and the last pre-war single deckers in the fleet. These – Bristol L5Gs – had the distinction of being the last vehicles to sport 'bible' destination indicators and whilst they might not have been mourned by the crews who had these heavy metal objects to handle, they nevertheless marked the end of an era.

Modifications made to the fleet during the year included the fitting of reversing lights and interior mirrors to EUG and SUG-type single deckers to make them suitable for one-man-operation and the partial blanking-off of the Cave-Brown-Cave air intakes of the Lodekkas fitted with this already troublesome equipment. Additionally, one of the 1950 L6B coaches – CB3 – was fitted with special side and headboards on its roof for use on the special airport service from Leeds to Leeds/Bradford airport operated under contract to B.K.S. Air Transport, the main airline serving this terminal. Coloured depot identification discs were introduced during April, these being fitted alongside the front and rear fleet numbers of all main fleet vehicles in order to assist traffic staff. As the colours represented only the main depots – sub-depots taking the colour of their parent – it was thought unnecessary to fit these discs to York West Yorkshire or Keighley West Yorkshire vehicles as these were already identifiable by the prefix letter to their fleet number. The colours used were: Bradford – blue, Harrogate – green, Keighley – grey, Leeds – maroon and York – yellow.

Although plans had been drawn up for the extensions to the company's central repair workshops at Harrogate and the new bus station and garage at Wetherby, these had to be deferred due to a BTC directive restricting expenditure. The provision of extra toilet facilities at Chester Street, Bradford and the extensions to Vicar Lane bus station at Leeds had however been completed. A further result of the spending cut-back was the reduction of the 1958 vehicle replacement order from 10 to 7 single deck vehicles, although the 2 Austin A30 staff cars were unaffected. Finally, the remaining plot of land at White Cross, Guiseley was sold in May to the Postmaster General and soon afterwards a new telephone exchange was built on this site.

Early the following year, a further property was purchased in East Parade, Harrogate and soon afterwards, upon hearing of the proposal to close Leeds Central railway station, the company made a tentative approach expressing interest in a portion of this site when it eventually came up for disposal. Being directly opposite Wellington Street bus station – which was already becoming overcrowded – the Central Station site was looked upon as being a useful extension to the existing premises, despite being at the opposite side of the road. Meanwhile, at Keighley, the joint company was negotiating for the purchase of certain properties adjacent to the Townfield Gate bus station to enable them to enlarge this, but here of course the Corporation were involved too. The plans for the extension of the body shop at Harrogate and the new premises at Wetherby were again resurrected and on this occasion were given approval and work was quickly put in hand whilst at Leeds, agreement was reached for the leasing out of the bus station kiosk and a lock-up shop near the company's enquiry office in Vicar Lane. Finally, at Harrogate part of the spare land behind Grove Park depot was sold to the owners of the adjoining factory towards the end of the year.

One of the sad occasions of 1959 was the closure on 4 April of the company's depot at Yeadon, which had also for many years

Based on an ex.War Department AEC Matador chassis, West Yorkshire's heavy recovery lorry 1022 had its new body built in the company's bodyshop at Harrogate in 1958 before its entry into the ancillary fleet. It carried an all-green livery.

Below: The summer and winter uniforms as worn in post war years prior to the NBC era.

CB3, one of the Bristol L6B coaches delivered in 1950 was fitted with special head and side boards for operation on the contracted B.K.S. service from Leeds to Leeds/Bradford airport in 1958.

Left: EUG74, a 1959 Bristol MW5G dual purpose single decker is seen here in Victoria Coach Station, London after operating a journey from Yorkshire during the busy summer months of 1960.

Below: After spending ten months in its striking black livery, double deck KSW coach 851 was repainted red & cream but at first retained its chrome-plated trim as shown here in 1954.

served as a store for redundant and surplus vehicles. The 10-vehicle allocation was divided between Leeds and Bradford depots, as were the services previously operated by the depot and after standing empty for a period of time, the whole of the property was sold to Aireborough U.D.C. in February 1960.

The intake of new vehicles during 1959 comprised 5 LD6B Lodekkas, one of which was the first bus in the fleet to be equipped with fluorescent lighting, and 10 MW5G dual-purpose vehicles, although of the latter, one did not enter service until the following year. In addition were 3 LD6B Lodekkas for the Keighley fleet. The 6 1950 Bristol L6B coaches were all down-graded to dual purpose status, changing their fleet numbers accordingly and compensating for this, the 6 half-cab L5G dual purpose single deckers were relegated to stage carriage work. Additionally, dual purpose LS5Gs EUG13-55 were all reduced ranks to stage carriage status, although in this instance no changes were made to either their seating or livery. Conversely, EUG56 upwards were all given a new predominantly cream livery to enhance their appearance when used on long distance services. More surprisingly, one of the Lodekkas – DX48 – had its Bristol engine replaced by a more powerful Gardner 6LX unit for evaluation purposes whilst the former double deck coach DBW31 was given a less-flashy livery. The old, and somewhat distinguished, underlined fleet name was superceded by one using letters of equal size and omitting the underline and this was applied to all the company's vehicles upon repaint.

The ancillary fleet also underwent change, the first of which was the conversion of the second Morris Commercial into a depot van. Later in the year, one of the ECW-rebodied pre-war K5Gs entered the body shop for conversion into a tree cutter, emerging in its new form in February 1960 when it replaced the Leyland TD2 which had carried out these duties since 1948.

Finally, the Fawdon Bus Company, in which West Yorkshire had held shares since pre-war days was voluntarily wound up on 24 July. The company's interest in the relative road service licences were however retained as a member of both the Yorkshire Services and the Northern (Limited Stop) Pools.

1960 began with the sale of their old depot premises at Yeadon as already mentioned and continued with the leasing out of another shop at Vicar Lane, Leeds and the first floor offices above their enquiry office. In order to improve the access at the north end of Harrogate bus station, a small plot of land adjoining the railway station was purchased from British Railways in September and on the 25th of that same month, the new bus station and garage at Wetherby was opened.

New vehicles joining the fleet comprised a trio of MW6G coaches, 9 of the new flat-floor FS6B-type Lodekkas and more surprisingly, a front entrance FLF6B Lodekka, this being the first forward entrance double decker ever owned by the company. York received 7 of the new FS6B Lodekkas whilst Keighley gained but 2 of this same type. The now customary down grading from coach to dual purpose and dual purpose to stage carriage status of several vehicles took place whilst some of the newer Lodekkas had their tungsten lighting replaced by that of the fluorescent type. Further new fitments introduced to the fleet were flashing direction indicators and within the next year or so, all the vehicles not due for early withdrawal were thus equipped.

Before leaving the year, mention must be made of the massive reorganisation of the Harrogate town services, many of those operating on a cross town basis exchanging their termini. This produced the first major change in the pattern of Harrogate's

West Yorkshire only purchased one front entrance Lodekka, an FSF6B which made its debut in 1960. Seen here in Otley bus station, it was later exchanged with United in 1967 for a rear entrance FS6B which also took fleet number DX82.

KSMA2, a Bristol SUL4A new in 1962 started life in the main company fleet and was transferred to Keighley West Yorkshire in March 1966.

One of a trio of MW6G coaches taken into the fleet in 1962, 1073 (originally CUG33) carried E.C.W. bodywork of a somewhat ugly design with shallow windscreens and a stepped waistrail.
(C. W. Routh)

routes for over thirty years and as a result of this reorganisation, many new housing estates gained a bus service for the first time.

The passing of another era was marked early in 1960 when the company finally withdrew the last of their Automaticket ticket machines from active service, replacing them with the 199 new Setright machines ordered during the previous year. Although once widely used by West Yorkshire, the Automaticket machines had only been used on special duties during more recent years.

1961 found another 39 vehicles joining the combined fleets with 16 FS6B Lodekkas, 6 MW6G coaches and 9 MW5G dual-purpose single deckers joining the main fleet and York and Keighley gaining 4 and 5 Lodekkas respectively. The York and Keighley buses together with the 5 most recent Lodekkas supplied to the main fleet were all fitted with T-shape front destination screens which displayed only a three-track route number and the ultimate destination and in addition sported a revised style of radiator grille.

Following completion of the extensions to the body shop at Harrogate's central works, attention was turned to the re-allocation of office space to the various departments using the company's head office in East Parade. Proposals were made for the conversion of nearby Westmoreland House to provide additional space, particularly for the engineering department and this work was put in hand later in the year. Following the ending of the previous tenancy of three properties in Little Horton Lane, Bradford, these were all re-leased to new occupants in November.

Few service changes of any note were made during 1961 save for an extension of the 32A Leeds-Yeadon route which was continued from Albert Square, Yeadon, to a housing area at Hawthorn Road on 3 July and the introduction of a new service from Shipley to Plumpton Lea, Wrose on 3 December. Numbered 64A, this must have been one of the shortest Lived of any West Yorkshire service, being withdrawn after only 16 days operation.

1962 saw the addition of the usual assortment of new vehicles, plus a type entering the fleet for the first time. For York and Keighley came 7 and 5 FS6B Lodekkas respectively whilst for the main fleet were 12 FS6B Lodekkas, 3 MW6G coaches and, 6 lightweight Bristol SUL4A 36-seaters. Powered by 4-cyl. Albion engines, these were bought primarily for use on rural services and had been ordered following the examination of a Western National example during the previous year. Amongst the vehicles replaced by the new arrivals were the last lowbridge Bristol K5Gs – post-war rebodied 1937/39 buses from the Keighley fleet which made their final journeys at the end of December. A more unusual purchase was that of 2 grass cutting machines for use at Grassington and Pateley Bridge depots, whilst following long deliberations by the BTC, the order placed in November 1961 for 14 double deckers; 10 single deckers; 6 coaches and 2 staff cars for delivery in 1963 was reduced a year later by 1 double and 1 single decker.

New vehicles arrived during 1963 at a rapid rate and before the year ended, no fewer than 52 had been received. These comprised 12 FS6B Lodekkas, 6 MW6G coaches and 20 MW6G stage carriage vehicles for the main fleet, 8 FS6B Lodekkas for Keighley and 6 lightweight SUL4A 36-seaters for York. The MW6G stage carriage vehicles were the first underfloor engined service buses to be bought by the company, all the earlier examples having been demoted from dual-purpose status. Such demotions still continued and the first of the LS6G coaches were down-graded to dual purpose roles (although they all retained their cream coach livery) and more dual purpose MW5Gs were relegated to stage carriage duties.

In an attempt to save on linen, the destination blinds were removed from the rear boxes of a number of rear-entrance single deckers, their screen glasses then being painted out red while in July a start was made in altering all the double deckers with full blind displays to screens of T-shape, showing only the route number and ultimate destination. This was accomplished by either panelling over the old aperture or in the case of older vehicles due for early withdrawal, painting out each end of their intermediate screens.

Towards the end of the year two of York West Yorkshire's Bristol L5G single deckers had their bodies removed in preparation for their conversion into towing wagons whilst another bus of the same batch was temporarily fitted up for towing duties at Leeds depot. The complete conversions involved shortening the chassis and building brand new bodies in the company's Harrogate body shop and it was September 1964 and August 1965 before they were completed and able to take up their duties at York and Keighley.

Grassington depot forms the backdrop for this view of SMG29 and SMG13, a pair of 1963 Bristol MW6G buses both of which are seen on routes serving the picturesque Yorkshire Dales.

FROM B.T.C. to T.H.C.

From the beginning of the year, the shareholdings of the British Transport Commission had been transferred to the newly-created Transport Holding Company and thus West Yorkshire had new masters yet again, even if in name only. During the spring, the Skipton to Bradley stage service of Ezra Laycock, Barnoldswick was taken over, although no vehicles were involved and Laycock continued his other services as usual. Earlier, on 5 January, the stage services of Hargreaves of Hebden were acquired (Hebden to Grassington and Hebden to Skipton) following the decision of this operator to withdraw from bus work and concentrate solely on the coaching side of his business. No vehicles were involved and the Hebden-Skipton service was integrated into West Yorkshire's existing operations.

Following its involvement in a serious accident on the A1 at Hatfield on 16 April whilst operating the London service, MW6G coach CUG12 was dismantled by the company. 1963 also saw the demise of the mobile information bureau, Bristol JO5G 1018 which despite having been replaced by a new trailer-type office in August of the previous year had remained in the ancillary fleet.

During September a plan was submitted for a proposed further extension to the company's central works at Harrogate which would provide accommodation on the ground floor for the relocation of the electrical repair department which was at that time located on the gallery of the chassis shop, and on the first floor for the conductors training school and uniform stores then housed at 9, Regent Parade (which would then become vacant and available for future development). The provision of a staff canteen was also included, but as is well known, this plan never materialised.

1964 saw the arrival of the company's first rear-engined single deckers of the Bristol RE-type, 3 of which were fitted with 54-seat stage carriage bodywork and 6 with ECW 47-seat express bodies. The latter arrived in May/October and were put to work on the prestigious London service. Also added to the fleet were 12 more FS6B-type Lodekkas, and 6 MW6G stage carriage single deckers; York and Keighley gaining 1 and 2 Lodekkas respectively. During the late spring/early summer, more of the older LS5G dual-purpose vehicles were reseated with 45 bus seats for stage carriage duties, but surprisingly the previously demoted coaches CUG1-6 were upgraded again from dual purpose to full coach status. Alterations carried out included the complete removal of the rear destination boxes and screens from some LL and LWL-type single deckers and at the same time the alteration of their front destination screens to a side-by-side display of the type used on the dual-purpose LS and MW vehicles. Many of the older single deckers had their rear luggage boots panelled over and, adding a touch of uncalled-for luxury, some Lodekkas received rear wheel trim discs. On the experimental side, Lodekka DX174 was fitted with single rear wheels for a short time, a similar experiment having been carried out the previous year on one of the MW6G single deckers.

As a result of the late delivery of new vehicles, 4 of West Yorkshire's 1949/50 Bristol K6B double deckers were transferred to York-West Yorkshire between August 1964 and February 1965, these being the first conventional lowbridge buses to be operated by the joint undertaking since the Leyland TD1s. Their stay in York lasted until the summer of 1966 by which time sufficient new vehicles had arrived, thus allowing them to be transferred back to the company for disposal.

Top: Keighley West Yorkshire Bristol K6B KDB30 has had its destination screen partly painted out to show only the ultimate destination and route number.

Above: Other double deckers had their front destination screens panelled over to 'T' shape styling as shown by Keighley West Yorkshire K6B KDB54 seen here whilst on loan to Yorkshire Woollen District on a local Dewsbury service.

The first Bristol RELL to enter the fleet did so in 1964. Numbered SRG1 it is seen here some ten years later working a school special duty.

Management changes saw the departure of the traffic manager, Mr. J. W. Lawrence on 31 October to take up the position of general manager of United Welsh and chief engineer Mr. M. T. Smith on 31 December to become assistant chief engineer of Bristol Commercial Vehicles Ltd. Their replacements were Mr. J. A. Talbot and Mr. B. T. Hancock who took up their duties on 1 December and the first day of 1965 respectively.

A new service was inaugurated on 28 September from Leeds to Red Hall Way whilst on the previous day the Farsley service had been extended from its terminus at South Drive to The Gardens. The next developments took place on 4 January 1965 when, as a result of the introduction of a new one-way traffic scheme in Leeds, a number of services had to be re-routed to reach Vicar Lane bus station. Three months later, on 22 March, a new service was started from Cookridge Street, Leeds to Arthington via Pool whilst during the spring, the Yorkshire-Torbay Pool was formed with its headquarters located at the company's head office. The members of the Pool were East Midland; West Yorkshire; East Yorkshire; Yorkshire Traction; Yorkshire W.D.: Yelloway, Wallace Arnold and J. W. Kitchin & Sons of Pudsey. Finally, a new local service in Wetherby from the bus station to Hallfield Lane was inaugurated on 30 September operating on Thursdays only with 2 return journeys. This must be one of the shortest routes in the company's history, having a running time of just 3 minutes!

Following further negotiations regarding land on the old Central railway station site at Leeds, the company felt that the capital outlay did not justify the continuation of their plans and instead signed an agreement with Leeds Corporation for the use on Saturdays from Whitsuntide to the end of September for the next three years of their Bean Ings Mills car park as an overspill area for the overcrowded Wellington Street coach station. In September, it was agreed to sell the garage premises at Edderthorpe Street, Bradford (taken over from Blythe & Berwick in 1928) to British Road Services who had been leasing it since the early 'fifties. Plans were also drawn up for the revised layout of Chester Street bus station at Bradford and work on this was started early the following year.

One of four Bristol LS-type coaches bought secondhand from Eastern National in 1965, CUG44 gave the company almost eight years service before being withdrawn in 1973.

The only dual door RELL to retain its centre exit to the end of its life was 1966 Show model 1223 which is pictured leaving New Park terminus on a Harrogate local service in March 1981.

On the vehicle front, a further 14 rear-engined Bristol RELL-type buses joined the fleet as did 13 more FS6B Lodekkas and another 6 lightweight Bristol SUL4As, with 8 more Lodekkas going to York. Further dual-purpose LS5Gs were re-seated and down graded to stage carriage status during the early part of the year and during 1965 the Cave-Brown-Cave fitted Lodekkas began to receive Darvic (plastic) scoops to their air intakes. A surprising loan took place during February when RELH dual purpose ERG6 and SUL4A SMA16 were both hired to Scottish Omnibuses for a period of two weeks. Both were used in service in Edinburgh during their stay, for evaluation purposes.

In the ancillary fleet, a secondhand long wheelbase Land Rover pick-up truck joined the two similar vehicles bought new in 1964 and also added to the 'green' fleet was a new Bedford TK stores lorry. Departing were the 19-year old Bedford O-type stores lorry, the Bristol GO5G towing lorry cut down from a York West Yorkshire bus in 1950 and the Bristol L5G stores lorry which began life as bus no. 145 in 1939.

The surprise of the year however was the purchase of 4 Bristol LS6B coaches from Eastern National in November. Two of these were 34-seaters of 1955 vintage whilst the others were a couple of years younger and were 39 seaters. Before entering service on 1 April 1966 all were re-engined with the Gardner 6HLW engines removed from withdrawn coaches CUG1-4 and the 34 seaters had their capacity increased to 39.

The order placed in November 1965 for 1967 delivery comprising 10 Bristol FS6B Lodekkas, 24 RELL buses, 3 RELH express, 3 MW coaches and 3 staff cars was revised in June 1966 to 34 RELL buses, 3 RELH express, 3 MW coaches, 4 Bedford VAM buses and 3 staff cars, but before the arrival of any of these, 10 FS6B Lodekkas, 5 RELH express, and 16 RELL stage carriage single deckers were added to the main fleet in 1966 plus 17 Lodekkas for York and 6 of this same type for Keighley. Of the York buses, 6 ordered under the 1967 replacement programme were taken from West Yorkshire's 1966 order, West Yorkshire ordering a further 6 RELL buses for 1967 in their place. Amongst the RELLs delivered to the company in 1966 was one of dual-door layout and this was displayed at the Commercial Motor Show in London during September before being delivered to Harrogate. Surprisingly, in February one of the SUL4A single deckers – SMA17 – had its Albion engine replaced by a Perkins 4-cyl. unit, resulting in it being re-numbered SMP17. Although at that time it was believed that this conversion was of an experimental nature, it retained its Perkins engine until finally withdrawn in October 1972.

What might have been. One of Ledgard's ex. London RT-type AEC's – a type which it was thought might survive under West Yorkshire ownership – but didn't – leaves Vicar Lane, Leeds on the jointly operated 33 route to Rawdon early in 1967.

Now able to compete again on the open market, Bristol Commercial Vehicles borrowed one of the company's RELL buses – SRG15 – for six weeks in January/February, using it as a demonstrator to no fewer than 17 municipal operators, 8 B.E.T. companies, 3 independents and 2 operators in Northern Ireland. At the other end of the year in December, dual-door RELL SRG23 was loaned to Bristol Commercial Vehicles for demonstration to Alexander Midland, Central SMT and Eastern Scottish. Finally, 4 Bristol SUL4A 36-seaters were sold to Keighley West Yorkshire on 1 March when 4 Bedford VAMs with 43-seat ECW bodywork were ordered for the main fleet as replacements. These of course did not materialise until 1967.

During 1966, a driver simulator was purchased and installed in the training school at Moss Grange, Harrogate and despite the company having standardised on the Setright ticket machine, on March 28 a new Almex machine was placed in use for experimentation.

Following lengthy negotiations with the Union, agreement was reached for the introduction of a 40-hour, 5 day week on 19 June, but following alterations to duty schedules, the staff at Leeds depot imposed a ban on standing passengers for a few weeks in July. Later in the year plans were approved for alterations at Knaresborough bus station and work began on this towards the end of the year.

Meanwhile, the company had been offered a 1963 Bristol RELH chassis with shell body which had been used by Bristol Commercial Vehicles for demonstration purposes. This was duly purchased in November and was despatched to ECW at Lowestoft where the necessary completion work was undertaken. After being equipped to full coach specification, it entered service with the company in March 1967.

As was now becoming customary, the order for 1968 delivery comprising 30 Bristol VR, 8 Bristol RESL stage carriage, 6 RELH coaches, 3 staff cars and 2 service vans was soon to be revised and amended to 24 Bristol VR double deck, 6 RELL single deck, 8 Bristol LH, 1 Bristol LHS single deck, 6 RELH coaches, 3 staff cars and 2 service vans. The ordering of a Bristol LHS is most interesting as this was never delivered and was not of a type which ever featured in the combined fleet.

Ex. Ledgard Roe-bodied AEC Regent V 1949U at Otley depot on the first day of West Yorkshire ownership has had its former owner's fleet name removed in readiness for the application of its West Yorkshire transfers.

Above: Only two ex. Ledgard coaches were taken into the West Yorkshire fleet. Both were Ford Traders with Duple bodywork. This view shows CF1 outside Harrogate depot in the summer of 1968.

At the end of the year, Mr. H. N. Tuff, who had been general manager since 1950, retired. His replacement was Mr. J. W. Lawrence, the company's former traffic manager who, except for the previous two years, had spent all his working life with

Right: A scene behind Otley depot showing ex. Ledgard Daimler DGW12 freshly repainted into red livery, AEC Regent V DAW8 still in its former owner's blue and West Yorkshire Lodekka DX35.

West Yorkshire. One of his first major duties upon his return was undertaken in May when he began talks with the Exors. of S. Ledgard of Armley, Leeds in respect of the purchase of that company's road passenger transport business. These talks were eventually concluded on 4 August when a purchase agreement was signed which would transfer all Ledgard's vehicles, services, goodwill and their Otley depot to West Yorkshire. Following this, negotiations immediately began with Leeds Corporation for the sale to them of three of the Ledgard services – Leeds-Pudsey-Bradford; Leeds-Hawksworth Road-Horsforth and Troydale-Calverley. These were duly sold to Leeds during September and after the transfer of Ledgard's licences on 4 October, the well-known independent was taken over on 15 October.

The 95 vehicle Ledgard fleet comprised mainly secondhand buses which had originated from Preston Corporation, Ribble and Bristol Omnibus (Leyland PD1s), and AEC RTs and RLHs and Leyland RTLs from London Transport and coaches from a variety of sources. At first it was planned that the AEC Regent Vs, 2 Daimler CVGs, some of the former London RTs, the Leyland Tiger Cub, AEC Reliance and 2 Ford coaches would remain in use with their new owner, but in the event only 10 Regent Vs, 2 Daimler CVGs and the 2 Ford Trader coaches survived. The other 81 vehicles, although taken into West Yorkshire ownership were all withdrawn from service on the night of 14 October and placed in store at various of the company's depots pending sale. The 12 retained double deckers, although still sporting their attractive blue & grey livery all had West Yorkshire fleet names and numbers applied on 15 October and thereafter continued to operate from Otley depot. With careful planning, it had been found that not all the remaining – and now withdrawn – vehicles needed to be replaced on a one-for-one basis and to meet their immediate requirements, the company returned to service a number of Bristol KSWs and

The bodywork styling was greatly improved on the final three MW6G coaches bought by the company. Dating from 1967, 1086 (formerly CUG46) is seen here in 1972 whilst still wearing its attractive cream & maroon livery.

The four E.C.W. Bedford VAM14 buses had an extremely short life, entering service in 1967 and being withdrawn four years later. SML4 is seen here in Rougier Street, York on rural service 88.

Following the first dual-door RELL which took its place in the fleet in 1966, a further five were delivered during the following year. 1238 (originally SRG38), like its four sisters, was eventually converted to single door configuration.

E.C.W.-bodied Bristol RELH6G coach 1017 in full C.A.G. corporate white livery rests outside Bradford depot after having returned from London on a 307 duty.

LWLs which had been kept in store for several months.

New buses taken into stock in 1967 comprised 21 Bristol RELL saloons (of which 5 were dual door variants), the 4 Bedford VAM buses, 3 MW6G coaches and 4 RELH coaches (including the one purchased from Bristol Commercial Vehicles in 1966). All were for the main fleet and on this occasion neither Keighley or York received any new vehicles.

One departure from the fleet was the front entrance Lodekka, DX82 which passed to United on 17 April in exchange for a conventional rear entrance FS6B of similar age. This surprisingly

Right: A pair of Bristol KSW6Bs at Shipley show the original rear destination layout of DBW11 together with the modified apperture of DBW20. Both were delivered with open rear platforms and had their doors fitted retrospectively in 1954/5.

The 'new' DX82, a former United FS6B which was gained in exchange for West Yorkshire's solitary front entrance Lodekka.

Awaiting disposal behind Skipton depot in November 1968 are Keighley West Yorkshire Bristol K6Bs KDB29 & KDB35 (note their different destination styles) and ex. Ledgard BCK633, a former Preston Corporation Leyland PD1 of 1947 vintage.
(M. Lockyer)

took the now vacant DX82 fleet number. A more unusual visitor to the company on 22 February was Bristol Omnibus Co's rear-engined VR double decker which was inspected by the engineering staff but was not used in service.

The chief engineer, Mr. B. T. Hancock left the company on 31 August to become chief engineer with Western National, his place at Harrogate being taken by Mr. W. G. Stephen on 1 October.

Before the year ended, a start was made on the repainting of the ex.Ledgard buses into West Yorkshire's colours and although this was continued at the rate of one each week, somehow ex.South Wales Regent V DAW4 escaped and was not thus treated until 18 May 1968. All the acquired buses still kept their Ledgard destination blinds, although new blinds showing the company's route numbers were eventually produced and fitted. Whilst most remained at Otley depot throughout their

Former Ledgard ex. South Wales AEC Regent V DAW2, now in standard West Yorkshire red livery, whiles away its final months on Harrogate local services in 1969.

Left: 1268 a flat-windscreened RELL6G with unmasked destination screen passes through York during the summer of 1974 after being repainted into corporate NBC livery.

short West Yorkshire lives, the 4 ex.South Wales Regent Vs moved to Harrogate on 1 March 1969 for use on town services. Their days were numbered however and the last of the Ledgard double deckers were withdrawn from service on 31 July of that year.

In 1968 a further 25 Bristol RELL saloons arrived together with 6 RELH coaches whilst the Keighley fleet also gained 2 new RELLs. For delivery in 1970, 34 more RELLS were specified, as were 6 RELH dual-purpose single deckers, but this was not approved by the THC and was subsequently reduced to 19 RELLs and 6 RELHs.

During the year a plot of land acquired with the Otley depot was sold to Otley U.D.C. whilst the depot itself underwent alteration and repair. A house owned by the company at Tewit Well Road, Harrogate was sold on 8 February, but more important was the proposal in August to sell the bus station and garage at Northway, Scarborough and to transfer the fleet to United's garage and operations to United's Valley Bridge bus station. The depot and bus station were vacated on 27 April 1969, the one allocated vehicle moving to its new home in United's premises and Northway was sold three days later. Other property moves included the closing of the Yorkshire W.D./ Hebble booking office in Bradford and its transfer to the West Yorkshire office which it then shared at Chester Street and the acquisition by the company of Yorkshire W.D's enquiry office in Leeds' Central Bus Station. A further property deal involved the purchase of two more premises in Wilton Street, Bradford in February 1969 and it was agreed that these would be demolished when they were vacated by the present tenant. At Harrogate, the lease of the old Bilton Motor Co. garage at Mornington Terrace which was still owned by West Yorkshire was renewed again to Whitley & Butterwick (Motor Services) Ltd. for a further period of 7 years from 1 July 1969.

Although it was now part of the world's largest bus company, West Yorkshire continued to carry out its duties just as it had always done and there was little or no sign of change visible to its vehicles or operations. The new rear-engined Bristol VRT double deckers entered revenue-earning service on the first day of the new year and by mid-November no fewer than 49 buses of this type were in use. Of these, 2 were allocated to the Keighley fleet and 10 to York. Another new type to make its debut was the lightweight Bristol LH 45-seat single decker. 26 were delivered of which 2 were for Keighley and 6 were transferred to the York fleet from the main company's order. More RELL saloons arrived – 11 for West Yorkshire and 3 each for Keighley and York – and a further 6 RELH6G 47-seat coaches were also received. An incredible 98 new vehicles had been added to the combined fleet during the year and this enabled the standardisation machine to gather even greater momentum. Eliminated totally were all the 14 vehicles taken over from the Ledgard fleet, the last remaining Bristol KSW & K5G double deckers and the LL5G and LWL-type single deckers whilst further inroads were made into the Bristol LS-type buses, coaches and dual purpose single deckers. The new VRs also allowed the first Lodekkas to be taken out of service, a type which had been the backbone of the company's prestige routes for more than a decade.

Below: The former Ledgard depot at Otley after modernisation with its travel office at the front of the forecourt.

The final two Ledgard vehicles had been the Ford coaches, one of which had been used on the York City Tour throughout the summer. This was sold early in October, its sister having gone during the previous month.

With so many surplus buses, the company was able to assist some of its new NBC neighbours and on 1 May loaned 4 of York's recently withdrawn highbridge K5Gs and 2 of Keighley's lowbridge K6Bs to Yorkshire Woollen District Transport who at that time were acutely short of double deckers. One of the York

Bristol VRT 1919 which made its debut in 1969 shows its new parentage by its side advert but still retains its fleet name in pre-NBC fashion.

buses was exchanged for another of the same type after four weeks and all 6 then on hire were sold to Yorkshire W.D. on 18 August. Another company to find itself short of buses was Hebble Motor Services of Halifax, and in order to ease their position, they hired 2 Lodekkas (DX53/7) from 15 November until 31 December. These were replaced by DX7/33 on the following day and both these buses continued to operate for Hebble until 3 May 1970, the day upon which West Yorkshire took over 3 of Hebble's services.

An incident on the main York road to the east of Seacroft on 7 July resulted in the total loss of SRG46, a two-year old Bristol RELL which was damaged beyond repair by fire following an electrical fault whilst on the Leeds – Scarborough service.

The charred remains of SRG46 after its disasterous fire in July 1969 whilst working the 43 service to Scarborough await their removal to Harrogate.

At Harrogate, the company's central workshops were kept fully employed not only with their normal overhaul tasks but also with the removal of Cave-Brown-Cave heating systems from more Lodekkas and the overhaul of a number of buses for Yorkshire Woollen District. After a six-month sojourn in the bodyshop, the converted Bristol LWL finally emerged in its new form fitted with a Gardner 6LW engine in place of its original Bristol unit and took up its duties as Leeds depot towing wagon in July, replacing Ford Canada 1001.

Fewer changes than had been made during the previous year to services were implemented although there was a general revision involving those serving Aireborough, and the Horsforth to Cookridge section of the once daily service from Bradford was abandoned.

During the following year the Leeds & Bradford Airport at Yeadon gained its first regular bus service when the 51 route from Bradford to Harrogate was diverted into the airport complex. At this same time its sister service, the 50 from Bradford to Yeadon was extended into a new housing estate at Westfield, a quarter of a mile or so from its former terminus at Kirk Lane bottom, and later in the year (30 November) a similar short extension was made to the 38A, continuing this from Red Hall Lane to Red Hall Vale. Of greater significance however was the acquisition on 3 May of three services previously operated by Hebble from Bradford to Bingley, Duckworth Lane to Bingley and from Bradford to Huddersfield. The latter which was operated jointly with Bradford and Huddersfield Corporations took West Yorkshire back to Huddersfield after an absence of more than thirty years, their service from Ilkley (joint with Yorkshire W.D.) having been discontinued in 1939.

On this same day (3 May) a new one-way traffic system was introduced in Harrogate and this caused a massive re-routing of services entering and leaving the town. The Leeds – Ripon service no longer called at the bus station on its outward journeys but only on its return to Leeds whereas all other out-of-town services now had to complete a circuitous tour of the town centre to reach the bus station.

After gaining three new services at the beginning of May, West Yorkshire withdrew from one of its unprofitable rural routes from 18 May when they passed their duties on the 27 from Pateley Bridge to Lofthouse and Middlesmoor to Longster Bros. of Pateley, from whom they had inherited them in July 1930. West Yorkshire continued to operate their Saturday workings on the 27 however, a day on which Longster's coaches were usually

Following its down-grading from coach to dual purpose status, EUG95 (formerly CUG20) had a red band added to its otherwise cream livery in 1969.

otherwise employed.

During the year, work had been steadily progressing with the rebuilding and enlarging of Keighley's Townfield Gate bus station. This was carried out in conjunction with a new shopping precinct and multi-storey car park on adjacent sites and upon completion, the new bus station was brought into use on 29 November – although the 'official' opening did not take place until 4 June the following year. For the first time, the bus station was large enough to accommodate all the town services as well as those of longer distances and minor route changes were made as a consequence of this. During September an offer had been received from a firm of private developers for the land owned by the company at New Brook Street, Ilkley and following protracted negotiations, this was eventually sold in March 1972.

When compared with the previous year, 1970 was quiet as far as new vehicles were concerned with only 14 Bristol RELL saloons and 6 REHL coaches being added to the main fleet. The latter were unusual in having Leyland engines rather than the more customary Gardner units and were immediately put to use on the company's prestigious London services. Keighley received 3 Bristol RELL saloons whilst York gained 8 more VRT double deckers. 1971 saw a further 3 RELL saloons added to the Keighley fleet and 26 join the main fleet. Of the latter, 12 were fitted with dual-purpose type bodywork (based on a bus shell with coach-type seating) for use on the company's East Coast services whilst 3 of the normal saloons had experimental Leyland 0.500 engines. York also gained a trio of new single deckers, these being of the short RESL type with seating for 47 passengers. Of the 1970 RELLs, those numbered upwards from SRG105 carried bodywork of a revised styling which incorporated double-curvature windscreens instead of the

Bristol LH6L LH2 seen here in Grassington still carried its depot allocation disc alongside its front fleet number when caught by the camera. The LHs were unusual in being delivered with cream window frames rather than having a cream waist band.

ERG10, a 1966 dual purpose Bristol RELH6G stands alongside CRL4, a 1970 RELH6L coach outside Grove Park depot, Harrogate. Despite their official status, the ERGs were frequently used on coaching duties. Note the cream-painted front bumper of CRL4.

previous flat type.

During the late evening of 13 October 1970, one of the company's Bristol RELL saloons – SRG78 – then barely two years old was severely damaged when it caught fire inside Bradford depot. Fortunately its chassis was repairable and after being rebuilt in the Myrtle Road workshops almost a year later, it was despatched to Eastern Coach Works at Lowestoft from where it emerged, complete with a new body in April 1972. In October 1970, one of the recently withdrawn Lodekkas (DX37) was converted into a permanent driver training vehicle, the first of its kind ever owned by the company who had previously used any bus not required for service on the day concerned, and similar conversions followed in 1971 and 1973.

1971 heralded the start of one-man double deck operation when on 18 April York West Yorkshire's route 4 was converted on Sundays. This was followed by several all-day routes on 9 May and at Keighley experiments were carried out during July on the service to Hebden Bridge. The old established service to the rural surrounds of Dick Hudsons, high on the moors above Bingley was cut back to terminate at Eldwick whilst unusually, a Ribble coach from the Morecambe service laying-over in Leeds had a regular 'fill-in' duty on the X35 express service from Leeds to the airport at Yeadon.

The first signs of National Bus Company parentage came in August when a new design of 'national' bus stop began to appear. This was soon to become a familiar sight everywhere across the country and slowly, in the years ahead, was to replace West Yorkshire's own cast metal bus stop flags which had been in use since pre-war days.

On the vehicle front, the down grading and reseating from dual purpose 41 to bus 45-seat of Bristol LS5Gs continued at pace whilst two of the newer LS dual purpose single deckers were given 6-cyl. Gardner engines in place of their original 5-cyl. units in a bid to improve their performance. The air suspension fitted to some of the REs and FS-type Lodekkas which had not been particularly successful was replaced by conventional springing and in preparation for further extensions to one-person-operation a number of single deckers were fitted with reversing horns. Another milestone in the company's history was the employment of lady drivers for the first time. The undisputed major occurrence of the year came in October when a massive vehicle renumbering scheme took place. In this, the class distinguishing letters disappeared and a new four figure system was introduced in connection with computerisation within the company. In this new scheme, the main fleet, Keighley and York vehicles were all identified by the prefix of their new number, '1' indicating a main fleet vehicle and '2' and '3' respectively relating to Keighley and York machines. All the ancillary vehicles, irrespective of ownership were given a '4' prefix. Insufficient new number transfers led to unusual sightings for a few months, although this had been resolved by the early part of 1972 by which time all the fleet correctly displayed its new numbers.

The final month of 1971 saw the introduction of a new service from Bradford to Brighouse which was jointly operated with Halifax Joint Omnibus Committee and covered parts of a former Hebble route. Similarly covering parts of another ex.Hebble service was a new route from Bradford to Bingley via Cullingworth.

1971 had proved to be an eventful year in a great many ways with several gains and losses to be recorded. From 1 April, the assets of NBC's Area Architects office at Sefton House, Rhyddings Road, Ilkley were transferred to the company, thus placing yet more property under West Yorkshire's control. Later, on 10 September it was reported that a row of 12 freehold cottages in Mowbray Square, Harrogate had been offered to the company, these being situated in the middle of the central works/head office complex and even though there was no proposal at that time to extend the central works, it was thought desirable that this offer should be accepted. Incredibly all but one of these cottages was at that time being occupied, the rent for each being a mere 88p per week!

At Leeds, the Corporation and a firm of property developers were proposing a plan which would include the company's Vicar Lane bus station, and after entering into preliminary talks, it was decided to seek advice from NBCs Property Committee. Still in Leeds, talks with the Corporation relating to the joint operation and pooling of services with Leeds City Transport had reached an advanced stage, and although there were still a number of points upon which agreement could not be reached, it was hoped to inaugurate the first joint arrangement before the end of the year. By this time of course, the Government's new Local Government Bill had already been published and it had been noted that the company's operating area would then be divided between West Yorkshire Metropolitan County and North Yorkshire County and that this would obviously create a number of difficulties.

Meanwhile, the NBC in their rationalisation plans instructed West Yorkshire to sell their shares in Blackpool Omnibus Stations Ltd. and in Omnibus Stations Ltd. to Ribble Motor Services and to Blackpool Omnibus Stations Ltd. respectively. In addition, they were directed to sell their entire shareholding in London Coastal Coaches Ltd. to the NBC and all these transactions were completed on 10 March 1972.

The other sale, which was also completed early in 1972 was that of land owned at Thorncliffe Road, Bradford to a Leeds property development company. This year also brought with it an unusual crop of service alterations, the first of which involved the Harrogate area where on 6 February a number of changes were made to the town routes. The next came on the last day of April when the Leeds-Otley-Ilkley service was extended through to Skipton and some limited stop operations were introduced between Otley and Bradford on the 53 route – these being renumbered X53. A new service was introduced between Ilkley and Ben Rhydding, numbered 63B, but this was to enjoy only a short life, being withdrawn on 2 September. Without doubt however, the startling news was that of the proposed introduction of a new hail-and-ride minibus service in Harrogate planned to start on 4 September. In the event, this did not begin until 30 October due to the late arrival of the buses with which it was to be operated. Using the title 'Chauffeur Coach', it was at first announced that this service would operate experimentally until 23 December, but such was its success that it was continued after this date. Designed to encourage shoppers to leave their cars at home and travel by bus, this was basically a door-to-door service. Five basic routes were operated, but by telephoning the company's Harrogate office beforehand, the bus would divert from its primary route and pick up as near the passenger's home as possible. Both the vehicles used on this operation – Deansgate-bodied dual purpose 15-seat Ford Transits hired from the Ford Motor Co. – were fitted with two-way radios to enable pick-up instructions to be relayed to the driver whilst on duty. As both these vehicles were required to maintain the service it was decided that a third should be hired to act as a spare. Eventually arriving on 27 November this differed from the others by being a Ford transit with Strachans 16-seat dual-purpose body and instead of being in West Yorkshire's NBC poppy red & white

The two Deansgate-bodied Ford Transit Chauffeur Coaches weave their way between the stalls in Knaresborough market place in 1973.

livery, was blue, carrying the lettering '16-seat Strachans Demonstrator'. Finding it hardly ever needed to be used, its hire was terminated on 2 January 1973.

Added to the fleet during 1972 were a further 24 Bristol RELL 53-seat saloons plus 2 RELLS and 4 RESLs for Keighley and 4 RESLs for York. Following a directive issued by NBC headquarters regarding a new corporate livery which was to be applied to all vehicles owned by NBC subsidiaries, Bristol RELH coach 1035 was duly repainted into National white and given its new 'National' fleet name in large alternate red and blue letters in August. During the following month, Bristol VRT 1949 became the first stage carriage vehicle in the fleet to carry the new corporate poppy red & white colours. Before entering service in its new livery it was sent to Aldershot for a week in connection with the filming of a 'commercial' which was later frequently seen on television. The remaining variation of the new corporate colours – the local coach half poppy red, half white livery – did not appear until December when Bristol RELH 1006 was so treated. Breaking away from the new NBC identity was Bristol VRT 1935 which, in November was repainted into an all-over advertising livery for Status Discount Warehouses, thus becoming the first vehicle to be transformed into a mobile advertising hoarding by the company. Being nominally a one year contract, this bus reverted to fleet livery in January 1974.

Further extensions to OMO brought the introduction of the farebox system. On this method of fare collection, passengers placed their coins for the exact fare into a box beside the driver, who was able to check this was correct before allowing it to drop into a sealed container. No change was given and at first no tickets were issued, although special tickets were introduced at a later date. York-West Yorkshire routes 4/4A were the first to be converted (on 26 March 1972) and for this purpose 12 VRTs were fitted with equipment hired from Setright. Following this new venture, Farebox operation was introduced to a number of town services in Keighley on 5 August 1973 when VRTs were again used.

1973 proved to be an eventful year in many ways, perhaps the most important of which was the winding up of Keighley West Yorkshire Services Ltd. As a result of the reorganisation of local authorities planned by the Government to take effect from 1 April 1974, it was realised that with Keighley becoming part of Bradford Metropolitan District from that date, the existing agreement between the company and Keighley Corporation

1340, one of a batch of dual purpose-seated Bristol RELL6Gs in predominantly cream livery leaves Bradford on its way to Blackpool in 1972.

would not be able to be continued on the same basis. The solution was for West Yorkshire to take over the Corporation interests in the fleet and garage in return for the transfer of the freehold of the bus station to the Corporation. Agreement was reached to this effect between the two parties at a meeting held on 12 November and Keighley West Yorkshire became a wholly-owned subsidiary of West Yorkshire as from 1 January 1974. Whilst Keighley West Yorkshire ceased to trade from 31 December 1973, the fleet remained intact and the fleet name soldiered on until September 1974 when it gradually began to disappear in favour of the West Yorkshire title. The transformation was slow however and it took until August 1975 to complete this task, Lodekka 2740 being the last vehicle to carry the Keighley name.

Across at York, the Joint Committee had already taken the decision not to fully implement NBC's policy regarding the corporate image and whilst it was agreed to alter the livery from Tilling red & cream to poppy red & white as and when vehicles were due for repaint, it was decided that the 'double N' symbol would not be applied nor would the fleet name be in NBC's new standard 5in. white lettering. Thus at least some of the old standards remained and the neat equal lettered gold fleet name soldiered on. More of the city's services underwent revision on 2 September and these involved further conversions to farebox operation.

The NBC corporate-style fleet name introduced in 1972 is shown here on the side panels of Bristol VRT 1904.

One of the first Leyland Nationals to enter revenue-earning service was 1415 which did so in August 1973, the month in which it was caught by the camera in Harrogate bus station.

The updating of the fleet continued with the entry into service of 22 Bristol RELL6G saloons and 5 new Plaxton-bodied 49-seat Bristol RELH6G coaches, these introducing a new coachbuilder to the company. More outstanding however was the delivery in July of West Yorkshire's first two Leyland Nationals. Being of the single door type with seating for 52-passengers, these were at first extensively used for driver training purposes and did not enter revenue-earning service until November. In the meantime 3 more had arrived and had taken up their duties on 1 August. A further 2 Nationals were received before the year ended, but both were retained in store for several months and did not enter service until May 1974. The remaining vehicles to make their debut in 1973 did so in December in the form of 2 Bristol LH6Ls with standard ECW 45-seat bodies. York received 5 more Bristol VRTs and 4 Leyland Nationals whilst Keighley added 5 Leyland Nationals to its fleet, these being the last buses to enter service with that company.

An unusual vehicle to join West Yorkshire arrived on 8 August on a four-week loan from Metropolitan Cammell Weymann of Birmingham. A Scania CR145-type chassis with ECW 37-seat luxury coach body complete with toilet, it was used by Leeds depot on the company's London service before being despatched to another NBC company for further evaluation. On the debit side, 2 of West Yorkshire's withdrawn Lodekkas (an LD6B and an FS6B) were loaned to United Counties Omnibus Co. Ltd. in October and were followed in November by 3 of Keighley's LD6Bs and an FS6B. In the event, none of these six buses ever returned to their rightful owners, all being sold by United Counties on West Yorkshire's behalf between November 1974 and March 1975. A further loan was made in November when Leyland National 1412 went to Grimsby Cleethorpes Corporation for two days for examination.

During the autumn at a time when the company's central workshops capacity was greatly stretched, a number of RELLs and a VR were contracted out for body repairs, 4 REs going to ECW and more surprisingly 2 REs and the VR being dealt with by Southfield Coachworks at Loughborough. A second all-over advertising bus made its debut in November when Bristol VR 1936 was given a predominantly white colour scheme for Buywell Discount Store at Thorp Arch.

On 1 October, responsibility for marketing and organisation of all NBC's express coach services was placed under the control of the newly created Central Activities Group. This meant that

An unusual mixture. West Yorkshire 1697 is seen here at Bedford bus station in December 1973 whilst on loan to United Counties. Still carrying its West Yorkshire fleet name, it has a side poster for Eastern National and is fitted with United Counties destination blinds which on this occasion are set to 141 Aylesbury.
(T.G. Walker)

West Yorkshire were no longer in control of their own express network but were merely contractors to National Travel and provided vehicles and crews as requested. Although they retained a great many of their old duties, some were inevitably lost to other NBC subsidiaries, especially the new National Travel companies created under this new edict.

Finally, production of West Yorkshire's timetable booklet in the form in which it had been presented since the 'twenties ceased and it was replaced by five (much slimmer) area volumes, the first of which appeared in November.

1974 witnessed the entry into service of the last Bristol RELLs to be purchased new. Arriving in October of the previous year, one was a Gardner-engined version whilst the other three had Leyland 0.600 power units. The latter never ran in this form however, exchanging their engines with the Gardner power

Bristol RESL6G 1103 squeezes its way over a swing bridge across the Leeds & Liverpool canal on its way from Riddlesden to Keighley in April 1976.

packs in three of the Plaxton-bodied RELH coaches before entering service in January and May. 14 more Leyland Nationals took up their duties during the year as did 4 LH6L saloons and a further 15 Plaxton bodied RELH coaches with Leyland engines. York received a mere 3 new buses, 2 Bristol VRT 74-seaters and a Leyland National. The arrival of so many new vehicles allowed the withdrawal of more Lodekkas and MW saloons, dual purpose vehicles and coaches and enabled several vehicles to be loaned to other NBC subsidiaries to assist with vehicle shortages at this time. 7 MW5G saloons were hired to West Riding at Wakefield from April/May, returning home between October 1974 and August 1975 whilst 5 RELL single deckers were loaned to United Counties from the end of May until July/August. The MWs never re-entered service with West Yorkshire while the REs resumed their duties immediately upon their return.

Originally a member of the Keighley West Yorkshire fleet, Bristol RESL6G 1108 was transferred to the main company upon the demise of the Keighley undertaking and is seen here at Greengates on the 760 service to Leeds in July 1979.

Another loan involved brand new Leyland National 1420 which operated for Derby Corporation's Blue Bus Service subsidiary at Willington from 5 to 26 February for evaluation purposes. Upon completion of this duty, it was placed in store ay Harrogate before finally entering service in May.

Following the reorganisation of Local Authorities and the creation of Passenger Transport Executives, the transport undertakings of Leeds, Bradford, Halifax and Huddersfield Corporations were all transferred to the newly formed West Yorkshire PTE on 1 April 1974 and although West Yorkshire Road Car Co. Ltd. were not directly involved in this, despite unsuccessful attempts by the PTE to purchase the company, their services operating within the PTE area were to be co-ordinated by this new body as part of their edict. This led later in the year to the introduction of the Metrocard travel pass which was available for use on all stage carriage services within West Yorkshire, irrespective of which company operated these. Another new ticket introduced, this time by the company in July, was marketed under the name 'Dalesrider'. This allowed one days unlimited travel on services to the Yorkshire Dales in addition to certain connecting services from most major towns served by the company and represented excellent value for money. In connection with the Dalesrider ticket a number of new services were inaugurated on Sundays and at holidays including Otley to Lofthouse and Harrogate to Bolton Bridge. Later in the year the normal stage services in the Baildon area underwent revision and a new Chauffeur Coach service was introduced on Wednesdays to serve Follifoot and Knaresborough Market.

After spending the majority of his working life with the company, J. W. Lawrence, the director and general manager retired on 30 September. Although it had been announced some six months earlier that Mr. F. E. Dark, general manager of West Riding would be his successor, in the event his replacement at the helm was Mr. R. H. Roberts who had previously held the position of general manager of East Midland Motor Services Ltd.

The corporate NBC image was now gaining momentum and as well as being visible on the company's vehicles it was now

Plaxton coachwork made its appearance within the fleet in 1973 when five Bristol RELH coaches were delivered. One of the following year's intake, 1054 on a South West Clipper duty illustrates the C.A.G. all-white livery.
(C. W. Routh)

1338, one of the dual purpose-seated RELL6Gs shows its corporate NBC local-coach livery and its windscreen-mounted pay as you enter sign as it leaves Leeds for Scarborough in 1974.

Crossing the Stray in Harrogate in the twilight of its life is Bristol RELL6G 1385 on local service 67A which in more recent times has been converted to Hoppa operation.

Below: Bristol LH6L 1177 receives attention on the vehicle lift in Roseville Road depot, Leeds in 1978.

beginning to show itself in other spheres. During August the 'double N' symbol was fitted to all the company's depots and travel offices and in July a new style of uniform for bus crews had been introduced. This was in a lighter material to that previously used and was in colour a greyish blue – and not nearly so smart as that formerly worn.

In addition to maintaining their own fleet, West Yorkshire also undertook work for some of their NBC neighbours and overhauled or repaired several buses for West Riding and Yorkshire Traction during 1974. In addition, they helped other NBC subsidiaries by supplying an assortment of mechanical and body spares including a number of Bristol engines removed from redundant Lodekkas to United. The old Tilling-style red & cream livery finally disappeared on 27 August when former Keighley Lodekka 1740 was withdrawn from service and the transformation to NBC's corporate colours was now completed. Similarly, the last bus fitted with tungsten lighting – York Lodekka 3689 – was also withdrawn during the year (on 30 June), thus ending a long era dating back to the early 'twenties.

A total of 14 new Leyland Nationals and a pair of VRTs joined West Yorkshire during 1975, as did a new Ford Transit pick-up truck whilst York gained 4 more Nationals and 2 VRTs. The York fleet which now required more double deckers was strengthened by the transfer of 8 Bristol VRTs from the main fleet between July and October in exchange for 3 Bristol RESL and 3 RELL single deckers. A point of interest relating to the new main fleet arrivals is that 3 of the Leyland Nationals and the 2 VRTs were ordered by Keighley West Yorkshire, although by the time they arrived, this company was no longer.

Few service changes of any significance took place during the year, although new routes were introduced between Bilton and Woodlands (a Harrogate local route) and from Leeds to Sunderland (joint with United). Two applications were made in June involving services in the Aireborough district when it was proposed to replace existing routes with a new Leeds to Westfield service running via West Park and Yeadon and from Bradford to Yeadon via Greengates and Henshaw. Before either were considered by the Traffic Commissioners, both applications were withdrawn however and the existing services continued unchanged. From 30 March, in connection with the Dalesrider operations, a new service was inaugurated from York to Ilkley via Harrogate, Fewston and Bolton Bridge and the 71 route from Skipton to Buckden was extended onwards to Arncliffe. These were followed in April 1976 by new Dalesrider Sunday only services from Pateley Bridge to Ripon via Studley Roger and from Harrogate to Skipton via Almscliffe Crag and Blubberhouses with additional routes being introduced in May from Bradford to Hawes; Bradford to Knaresborough; Bradford to Pateley Bridge via Appletreewick and from Keighley to Pateley Bridge. These ran each Wednesday and Sunday and also on Mondays and Tuesdays during the Leeds, Bradford and Keighley holiday weeks and proved extremely popular with passengers wishing to get away from the towns for a day and enjoy the beauty of the Yorkshire Dales.

Among the vehicles of other NBC subsidiaries which received attention in West Yorkshire's workshops was Yorkshire Traction Atlantean 612, seen here leaving Grove Park depot, Harrogate on West Yorkshire trade plates.

Following the introduction of service co-ordination and rationalisation by West Yorkshire PTE, all the company's services radiating from Leeds, Bradford, Keighley, Otley and Ilkley were renumbered on 23 May into a common series covering the whole of the county. Most were placed in the 600 and 700 series and the renumbering eliminated the use of suffix letters such as A, B, C etc. All the company's services were now incorporated to the PTE's area timetable booklets which in turn replaced those issued by the company for Leeds, Bradford and Keighley, leaving only the York and Harrogate & Dales area booklets as the responsibility of West Yorkshire.

The end of an era was marked on 7 February when the last portable post box in the north east was carried by a company vehicle (on the Harrogate – Pateley Bridge service). Late post boxes had been carried on West Yorkshire vehicles since the 'twenties and although latterly placed inside the vehicle, they had in earlier years been attached externally to the front bulkhead above the front nearside wing and indeed until 1940 most new buses purchased by the company incorporated special attachments for this purpose.

Further consolidation was achieved on 25 May when the company took over two local services in the Skipton area previously operated by Ribble to Eastby and Bolton Abbey. No vehicles were acquired with this transfer, although Ribble had offered a pair of Leylands which were declined due to them being non-standard to the West Yorkshire fleet. Although Ribble continued to operate their longer services from Skipton to Lancashire, they closed their depot in the town at this same time, moving their small vehicle allocation to the West Yorkshire depot where minor alterations had been undertaken for this purpose.

During the year the fleet was further enhanced by the arrival of 8 more Leyland Nationals and their first Leyland Leopard coaches, these being fitted with Plaxton 49-seat bodies. Also new were 3 Leyland-engined Bristol VRTs, although these, instead of entering service, went direct to Trent in September/October and did not arrive at West Yorkshire until 1 January 1977. York however received their 2 new VRTs on 1 October. In addition to the usual exit of Lodekkas upon receipt of the new arrivals, the first of the company's RELL saloons were withdrawn, despite not yet being twelve years old. Comparatively new Leyland National 1456 was extensively damaged in an accident in Kirkstall Road, Leeds on 1 June, having to be returned to Leyland's 'hospital' at Chorley for rebuilding whilst on 22 November, Lodekka 1824 sustained sufficient damage at Cononly where it ran into a house, to cause its premature withdrawal. An even greater fate befell Trent Motor Traction on 13 July however when a disastrous fire swept through their Derby depot destroying or severely damaging almost 50 buses. Answering their call for help, West Yorkshire early the following morning despatched 5 Lodekkas and 1 RELL saloon to Derby to assist Trent to maintain their serices. The RELL was returned the same day due to the prime requirement being for double deckers, but the Lodekkas remained until the end of the month (3) or the end of August (2). Prior to this, West Yorkshire had

1784 was one of the vehicles sent to Derby to assist Trent after their disastrous depot fire. Pictured in Derby bus station on 21 July 1976 it is in the company of Derby Corporation and Trent buses.

sold 6 Lodekkas to United for use at Scarborough during the busy summer season. A further loan made during 1976 was that of Leyland National 1467 to East Yorkshire Motor Services on 26 May for driver training purposes. In exchange, East Yorkshire provided the company with a Marshall-bodied dual purpose Leyland Leopard which after a week or so was replaced by another vehicle of the same type which remained with the company until 1467 was returned in July.

Meanwhile, West Yorkshire made a start on the conversion of their 3 Leyland engined RELL saloons to Gardner power units and 2 were so treated in June and September, the third being thus re-engined in February 1977. The final occurrence of 1976 involved Bristol VRT 1946 which in December was sent to Northern General's workshops to be sprayed into a silver livery with purple relief band at upper deck floor level in preparation for H.M. Queen Elizabeth II's Silver Jubilee celebrations during the following year. Sponsored by Camerons Ales, 1946 returned to West Yorkshire in its striking new livery during the final few days of the old year. After operating from various of West Yorkshire's depots during the first six months of 1977, it was loaned to United at their Middlesbrough depot from 14 July to 5 August and again from 18 August to 1 December in exchange for a United VRT painted in an all-over advertising livery for Camerons. Earlier in

Painted in a special silver livery for the Jubilee of H.M. Queen Elizabeth II, Bristol VRT 1946 is seen here in Middlesbrough whilst on loan to United. In its place, all-over advertising liveried United 686 was loaned to West Yorkshire. It is pictured here at Shaw Estate, Yeadon on 24 August 1977.

the year, on 28 February, another VRT, 1949 which had been fitted with an experimental transmission system, also spent some time on loan to United, returning to Harrogate on 16 June, but on this occasion, no vehicle was received in exchange, instead York West Yorkshire VRT 3974 being transferred to Harrogate depot to maintain its vehicle strength.

New vehicles taken into stock comprised 17 Leyland Nationals; 10 Bristol VRTs; 4 Plaxton-bodied Leyland Leopard coaches and 3 Leopards with Duple dual purpose bodywork for the main company together with 7 VRTs for York. Added to the ancillary fleet were 2 vans, one being a Ford Transit, the other a Ford Escort. Further additions were made in October when, surprisingly, 6 secondhand coaches were acquired from Midland

One of the Bedford coaches acquired from Trent, 2104 passes through the wash in Grove Park depot, Harrogate in June 1979. Parked in the back corner of the depot is baby National 1001.

Refurbished by Willowbrook who fitted a revised style front end to its E.C.W. dual purpose body, Bristol RELH6G 1025 rests on the forecourt of Harrogate depot in 1978.

General. These were all Bedfords, 2 being VAM70s with Duple coachwork, the remaining 4 being YRQs with Plaxton bodies. All were stored at Harrogate pending their entry into service in the spring of 1978. The engine changing programme was completed when Bristol RELH coaches 1038/9 gave up their Gardner units in favour of Leyland 0.680 engines at the end of February.

Once again faced with a backlog of work, the company's central bodyshop at Harrogate could not keep pace with the fleet's needs and in January a contract was signed with Willowbrook under which a number of RELL saloons and dual purpose single deckers were to receive attention. This involved the strengthening of the front end of their bodies and it was more than a year before all the vehicles contracted were completed. In addition, one of the RELH dual purpose 47-seaters of 1964 vintage was also despatched to Willowbrook's Loughborough workshops for rebuilding and modernising. After spending almost eight months away from home, it eventually returned with a completely re-styled front end and, before re-entering service it was modified by the company from manual to semi-automatic transmission.

Operationally, 1977 proved to be a year of many changes, the first of which occurred on 1 January when, following the change of ownership of Longster Bros. of Pateley Bridge, the company regained the Pateley – Lofthouse service, thus completing the circle. On the following day three new services were introduced between Bradford and Skipton (via three different routes) to provide a 20-minute frequency between these towns and replacing the existing services and also a new through service was commenced between Bradford and Mytholmes via Keighley and Haworth. This too had a 20-minute frequency and between the above, there was a bus between Bradford and Keighley every 10 minutes. A couple of months later, on 27 April, the new transport Interchange at Bradford was opened. Having been built at a cost of more than £16 million, it included a railway station, bus station and an underground garage in which 200 West Yorkshire PTE vehicles could be housed. All West Yorkshire's operations serving Bradford were moved into this new building and their bus station and travel office at Chester Street duly closed on the previous night.

Following three years of meetings between West Yorkshire PTE and the various NBC subsidiaries operating into the county, the formation of a new joint company under the title of Metro-National was approved, the function of which was to control all local services and avoid duplication of routes and operating schedules. Although it was expected that the new joint company would come into being on 1 July, it was not until 1 January 1978 that it finally became operative.

As an addition to the successful Dalesrider operations, the PTE evolved a network of services under the Parklink banner to encourage people to visit the National Park areas of the Yorkshire Dales at weekends and during the summer months. In support of this, from 11 June West Yorkshire extended several journeys on their 71 service from Buckden to Skipton railway station to connect with trains from Leeds and Bradford etc.

Operations on the Bradford-Keighley/Haworth services via Denholme were severely disrupted on 10 November when a land slip near Cross Roads resulted in the closure of the road. The only diversion possible was over a stretch of bleak moorland along narrow roads with one particularly tight corner. This precluded the use of normal 36ft. long Bristol RELLs or Leyland Nationals and double deckers and in order to be able to maintain their services along this temporary diversion, the company hastily transferred a trio of shorter RESLs to Bradford depot for these operations. Despite every effort being made by the local authorities it was during the week preceding Christmas before a temporary road could be laid and the normal route was able to be resumed.

1978 marked the Golden Jubilee of West Yorkshire Road Car Co. Ltd. (if its predecessors were to be ignored), and to commemorate the occasion a Leyland National – 1473 – was repainted in February into a special livery of gold and blue, being specially lettered to mark the jubilee. This spent time at all the company's main depots during the year until December when it was returned to normal fleet colours.

New services were introduced on 11 May when the Skipton local to Greatwood Avenue was replaced by a new route to Horse Close Estate and the Pateley Bridge to Middlesmoor

2527, a 1973 dual-purpose Plaxton-bodied Bristol RELH6L

The export of former company buses continued even after the boom period of the early 'fifties. Here, former York West Yorkshire YDX132, still in original livery and complete with fleet names and numbers is seen in Holland in 1976 under the ownership of Kleyn Trucks.

service was extended from Pateley through to Skipton. Later in the year, on 15 October there was a general reorganisation of the Keighley town services when OMO Autofare was extended to more routes. Meanwhile, proposals were made by the PTE to build a new bus station in Leeds in the markets area which would replace all the existing bus stations including those owned by the company at Vicar Lane and Wellington Street. To date this scheme has never come to fruition, and indeed in 1986 West Yorkshire stated that if it ever did, they would be totally against moving their services from their established terminal points. During May building was started on the extension of Myrtle Road works at Harrogate to provide a new stores area and this was completed by the end of the year.

Following Mr. R. H. Roberts' appointment as Group Executive for NBC's Northern Region from 1 August, Mr. B. M. K. Horner joined the company on 1 October as its new general manager, having previously served in a similar capacity with East Yorkshire Motor Services Ltd.

Delivered during 1978 were 4 more Leyland Nationals, 23 Bristol VRTs, 2 Leyland Leopard-Plaxton coaches, 8 Leopard-Plaxton dual purpose single deckers and 3 B-series short Leyland Nationals with seating for 44 passengers. No new buses were added to the York fleet on this occasion.

Following a comparatively quiet year, 1979 saw an unusual amount of changes to the fleet with both new and secondhand vehicles being added. Those new to the main company comprised 8 Leyland National 52-seaters; 11 'baby' National 44-seaters; 14 Bristol VRTs; and 6 each dual purpose and coach-bodied Plaxton Leopards whilst for York were 4 VRTs. Purchased secondhand were a trio of Bristol LH6L saloons from United, these arriving in March/April. Of these, the life of one was to be very short, it being withdrawn after less than three weeks in service whilst the others lasted somewhat longer until the end of May and October. These were but the tip of the iceberg however for continual vehicle shortages throughout the

Finished in corporate NBC-style red & white dual purpose livery is 2552, a Duple-bodied 49-seat Leyland Leopard.

year brought many strangers to the company's midst. First to arrive were 5 Plaxton-bodied Leopard coaches from Ribble and a pair of Bristol FS5G Lodekkas from Lincolnshire. These made their debut between 23 January and 3 February, 3 of the Leopards and the two Lodekkas being allocated to York depot, the other 2 Ribble Leopards going to Leeds. Of the latter, one was never used and returned to its owners in March. One of the two Lincolnshire Lodekkas departed back to its home base on 13 March due to the expiry of its certificate of fitness and was replaced by a similar vehicle which, with its sister continued to operate in York until May. The Ribble Leopards began to leave for home between June and August whilst during the second week of July, 3 FLF6G Lodekkas and a pair of Willowbrook 49-seat Ford R1114 buses had been hired from Trent and 2 FS5G Lodekkas and 1 Ford R192 with Plaxton 41-seat coach body were taken on loan from Lincolnshire. All these were employed at Leeds depot and remained with the company until September. Meanwhile Bradford depot found itself acutely short of buses early in September and to overcome this 3 Bristol FLF6Gs were

Leyland National 1473 wqas painted into a special gold, blue & white livery to commemorate the Golden Jubilee of West Yorkshire Road Car Co. Ltd. in 1978. It is seen here in Colne bus station whilst working on the Keighley service.

One of the Leopard coaches hired from Ribble in 1979 stands in Leeds Vicar Lane bus station alongside one of the Willowbrook-rebuilt E.C.W.-bodied Bristol RELH6Gs.
(D. Akrigg)

Bristol LH6L 1161 stands alongside one of the Bristol Lodekkas hired from Trent in July 1979 in this Vicar Lane bus station scene, Leeds.

Brand-new United 3100, a 1979 Leyland National was borrowed by West Yorkshire for three months during the summer of that year. It is seen here in Harrogate on Ripon Road whilst working on local service 52 to Carmires Avenue. As will be noted, no fleet name or number is carried.

hired from West Riding, a Bristol RELL6G saloon from Northern General, an Alexander dual purpose bodied Leopard from East Yorkshire and 3 single deckers were borrowed from United – 1 RESL saloon, 1 RELL dual purpose and 1 RELH dual purpose, all with ECW bodies. All of these were used on all day stage duties by Bradford depot and remained with the company for around four weeks. Following the great variety of buses which had been seen around the company's territory for most of the year, it came as no surprise when on 12 September West Yorkshire purchased 10 single deckers from United. 8 of these were 46-seat Bristol RESLs whilst the remaining 2 were dual purpose 50-seat ECW-bodied RELL6Gs. All were immediately placed in service still in their United livery, albeit with West Yorkshire fleet names. A further hiring from United took place on 17 July when a new Leyland National was received and placed in service at Harrogate. This quickly returned to its owners on 22 July to help out after that company's Durham depot fire but was back in Harrogate three days later where it remained until October.

During the year the five E-registered dual door Bristol RELLs were all converted to single entrance 52-seaters, this task being completed in August leaving only 1223 in two-door form. Less pleasing was the loss of Bristol VRT 1715 on 13 May when its body was destroyed by fire in Vicar Lane bus station, Leeds. After its chassis had been rebuilt in the company's Myrtle Road workshops, it was despatched to ECW in August for fitting with a brand new body, arriving back in Harrogate on 5 November. Another accident victim was seven month old baby National 1010 of Malton depot which ran off the road at Sherburn near Scarborough on 21 November. The severity of the damage caused it to be returned to Leyland's Chorley 'hospital' for repair and it was not until May 1980 that it took up its revenue-earning duties once again.

The year started with floods in York followed on 2 January by 21 degrees of frost which resulted in 48 of the depot's 112 buses being off the road with frozen brakes and fuel pipes etc. This caused all York's cross-city bus services to be withdrawn for the following three days during which only skeleton services could be maintained. By 6 January however, sufficient buses had been returned to traffic to enable normal services to be resumed.

A reorganisation of services in Harrogate took place on 22 April which included the Chauffeur Coach routes whilst later in the year on 24 September extensive changes were implemented on the Leeds – Otley – Ilkley – Skipton corridor. Under these came a new service from Leeds to Otley via Holt Park Shopping Centre and a new limited stop commuter service from Addingham to Leeds via Otley. Three days later, proposals were announced by Metro National for a reorganisation of services in the Shipley area in which the joint PTE-West Yorkshire services from Bradford to Eldwick would be replaced by extensions to the PTE only services 624/5, the X67 Bradford – Keighley limited stop service would be withdrawn, the Hirst Wood to Wrose service would be replaced by PTE services and some services would be re-routed. In the event, these changes did not take place until 22 June 1980.

After such an extraordinary year as 1979, one wondered what the first year of the new decade would bring. This soon started to be revealed when on 7 January a number of services in West Leeds were revised. A new route from Leeds to Aberford via Crossgates was introduced as was a new circular service from Leeds via Crossgates and Scholes whilst the existing Leeds to Red Hall route was extended to a major new housing development at Whinmoor. Three more Dalesrider services began on Good Friday from Harrogate to Pateley via Fountains Abbey; to Pateley via Almscliffe Crag and from Harrogate to

1979 was a year of acute vehicle shortages within the company and to compensate, several single and double deckers were hired in the early autumn from a variety of NBC companies. Seen here are United Bristol RELH6G in Bradford Interchange and a West Riding FLF-type Lodekka (548) at Baildon Green on service 661.

Ilkley via Fewston and Askwith and on 31 October the joint service with Burnley & Pendle from Keighley to Colne was extended to Padiham.

New vehicles to arrive comprised 5 baby Leyland National 44-seaters; 13 B-series 52-seat Leyland Nationals; 21 Plaxton dual purpose-bodied Leopards and 11 Bristol VRTs. The long

One of the ex.Ribble short Plaxton-bodied Leyland Leopards, 2101 rests in the Bradford Interchange in March 1983 between its contract duties.

Mansfield District 141, one of the VRTs hired by West Yorkshire in 1980, approaches Bradford Interchange on a 667 duty from Keighley. (K. A. Jenkinson)

B-series baby National 1012 at York railway station in October 1982 was unusual in not having its white band extended across the front. It would appear that the band was peeling badly along the sides too.

2567 was adorned with a special promotional livery in the autumn of 1980 for use on the Leeds – Manchester – Liverpool service. A Plaxton-bodied Leopard, it was later joined by a Willowbrook version for the same service.

Nationals were delivered in all-over red livery with no white relief band and entered service in this fashion. For the York fleet came 7 new Bristol VRTs. These replaced various Bristol REs and the last of the Lodekkas (the last main fleet examples being withdrawn on 28 June followed by the final York FS6Bs on 30 November).

A temporary vehicle shortage at Keighley depot caused more hirings during March when 2 Lincolnshire VRTs and 2 Mansfield buses of this same type were taken on loan. The Lincolnshire pair returned home at the end of the month whilst the Mansfield VRTs stayed until 17 May. Another stranger to the company's fleet was a United driver training Lodekka which was borrowed from early March until 10 April to cover for one of the company's own Lodekka trainers which was receiving a new engine at that time.

Six of the Plaxton-Leopard coaches were upgraded during May for use on special private hire duties, being fitted with side curtains and carpets for this purpose. These extra luxury fittings were not retained for long however and were removed before the end of the year.

To compensate for the withdrawal of York's final Lodekkas, 8 Bristol VRTs and all 6 Bristol LHs, 13 Bristol RELLs (including the 5 converted from dual door) and 2 Bristol VRTs were transferred to York from the main fleet between August and December, thus providing the York fleet with more single deckers than it had ever owned since its formation in 1934. Joining the main fleet during the latter part of the year were a pair of secondhand Plaxton-bodied 43-seat Leopards acquired from Ribble for use on contracts from Bradford depot which required shorter vehicles.

The withdrawal of the Chauffeur Coach services in Harrogate in March resulted in the demise of the 2 Ford Transit minis which after a short spell at Keighley were placed in store whilst Leyland National 1418 suffered extensive damage after overturning in Thornton Road, Bradford on 16 September, causing it to be written off.

Before the year ended, the company received 9 new Leyland Leopard chassis which were to be bodied by Willowbrook. This coachbuilder had got so far behind with its production however that it could not accommodate any further chassis and thus West Yorkshire had to store these themselves. After remaining on the company's premises for some six months, and realising that Willowbrook were still unable to give a date when these chassis could be bodied, the order was transferred to Duple at Blackpool and all 9 were moved to their factory during May. The first arrived back, complete with its new 49-seat dual purpose body towards the end of July with the others following over the next couple of months. Joining them during 1981 were 3 Duple coach-bodied Leopards; 17 Leyland National B-series 52-seaters and 10 Bristol VRTs, these being the last of this type to be purchased new. Willowbrook did manage to supply 6 dual purpose bodied Leopards early in the year and for the ancillary fleet came 2

One of York West Yorkshire's Olympians, 3935 passes the railway station in February 1984 when only a few days old. As can be seen, it carries both the NBC symbol and York coat of arms alongside its fleet name.

Duple-bodied Leyland Leopard coach 2387 stops outside York railway station after finishing its duty on the 730 Torbay service in April 1983.

Transit pick-up trucks. York also received its last new VRTs with the delivery of 5 examples, although a further 2 had been acquired secondhand from the main fleet on 1 March.

Rather than having to hire any vehicles during 1981, the company were able to lend some to South Yorkshire PTE who had had a large number of vehicles removed from service following an inspection by the Department of Transport examiners. In mid-March 4 withdrawn VRTs from the main fleet and 2 from York were sent to Sheffield to help out, returning early in April.

The ancillary fleet which had sported a green livery since the mid-'fifties began to be repainted into poppy red at the start of the year whilst in August 3 Bristol VRTs received all-over advertising liveries – 1 for Morrisons Supermarkets, the other 2 for National Holidays. A month later Leyland National 1520 was given a Polybus advertisement for the Happy Eater Restaurant. Following the application of a special livery to Plaxton-Leopard 2567 towards the end of 1980 to promote the Leeds-Liverpool service, one of the Willowbrook-Leopards was similarly treated, this enhancing its appearance somewhat.

The most important event of 1981 took place on 26 April when the York M.A.P. scheme was implemented. This involved a massive reorganisation of the city's service network and took buses into many housing developments on the fringe of the city which had previously never enjoyed the benefits of the public transport system. At this same time the familiar gold York West Yorkshire fleet name carried by all the Joint Committee's buses was replaced by the title 'York' which was preceeded by the NBC 'double N' symbol and followed by the city coat of arms. Few of the main company's services saw major change, although there were a few alterations to those operating locally in Harrogate on 20 September.

During the late summer, all the company's stage carriage vehicles operating from depots within the West Yorkshire P.T.E. area had their conventional fleet names replaced by the corporate Metrobus name (which incidentally was also applied to the entire West Riding and Yorkshire fleets and some of Yorkshire Traction's buses). This created problems with future inter-depot transfers as the company's North Yorkshire depot's vehicles continued to feature the customary West Yorkshire fleet name.

1982 began with a new Thursday only service being introduced from Leeds to Boston Spa via Lingerfield and Wetherby which was to operate for a 6 month experimental period. Later, on 1 July the joint Burnley & Pendle service from Keighley to Padiham was extended yet again, this time to Accrington whilst in May the company made its debut in the continental tours market with a 3-day excursion to Holland. As an indication as to the direction the company intended to progress in the leisure market, the tours and excursion office in Low Harrogate was renamed Montpellier Travel during the spring. A major task placed upon the company was the co-ordination of transport for the Pope's visit to York on 29 May. This involved close liaison with numerous operators as well as the provision of vehicles from their own fleet, but as always, the job was carried out with total efficiency and smoothness.

Wearing unrelieved NBC poppy red livery, Leyland National 2 1533 with Metrobus fleet names prepares to enter the Bradford Interchange in November 1986.

Recently renumbered from 2391, 2613 is one of only three ECW-bodied Leyland Leopard coaches operated by West Yorkshire.

The intake of new vehicles was minimal during 1982 with only 5 B-series 52-seat Leyland Nationals and three ECW-bodied Leyland Leopard 49-seat coaches being purchased. For the ancillary fleet came a Transit van and a pick-up truck of the same type whilst a secondhand Atkinson tractor unit was also bought for conversion to a recovery vehicle. No new buses were bought

The new Metrobus fleet name which in September 1981 began to be applied to all the West Yorkshire buses based within the P.T.E. area

New Leyland Olympian 1820, running on trade plates, travels on Roseville Road, Leeds whilst being used for driver familiarisation on 30 April 1983.

for the York fleet, but instead a pair of secondhand Bristol VRTs were purchased from East Midland on 1 March, these being some seven years old. Four months later, on 1 July, York's first 4 Leyland Nationals, now surplus to requirements were transferred to the West Yorkshire fleet.

The hiring of buses from other NBC operators had now almost become an annual event, and 1982 was no exception. Arriving in June were 3 Bristol VRTs from Southdown and 3 buses of the same type from Mansfield District. All were sent to York where a shortage of double deckers was being experienced and the 6, still in their owner's green livery all took up their duties on 1 July. Eleven days later, a luxurious M.A.N. SR280 49-seat coach complete with servery and toilet arrived on loan from Trathens for use on the new Rapide service from Harrogate to London, this being necessary due to West Yorkshire having no suitably-equipped coaches themselves. This coach was replaced from time to time by other M.A.N's from the Trathen fleet to enable maintenance to be carried out and was finally returned to its owners on 7 October. Its replacement arriving the following day was a Duple Goldliner III-bodied Volvo B10M from Parks of Hamilton which was similarly equipped and this remained with the company until the last day of the year. Meanwhile, further vehicle shortages led to the hire of 3 more Bristol VRTs on 1 September, these coming from APT of Lincoln. Originally Midland General/Trent buses these were used at Keighley and Harrogate depots until their return to Lincoln at the end of the year. The Southdown trio were also sent home at the end of December, as was one of the Mansfields, leaving only 2 Mansfield District buses on hire at the start of 1983. By this time they had moved to Keighley depot where they stayed until their departure back to their owner on 17 April. More unusually, a Crosville LD6G Lodekka converted for tree cutting duties was borrowed from 20 August to 14 October and again from 25 October to January 1983. During its stay it was involved in tree pruning on the Harrogate – Pateley Bridge and Skipton – Grassington routes upon which it was intended to introduce double deckers in 1983.

1716 displays its wrap-round advert for Barratt Homes as it rests in the yard behind Otley depot in September 1980.

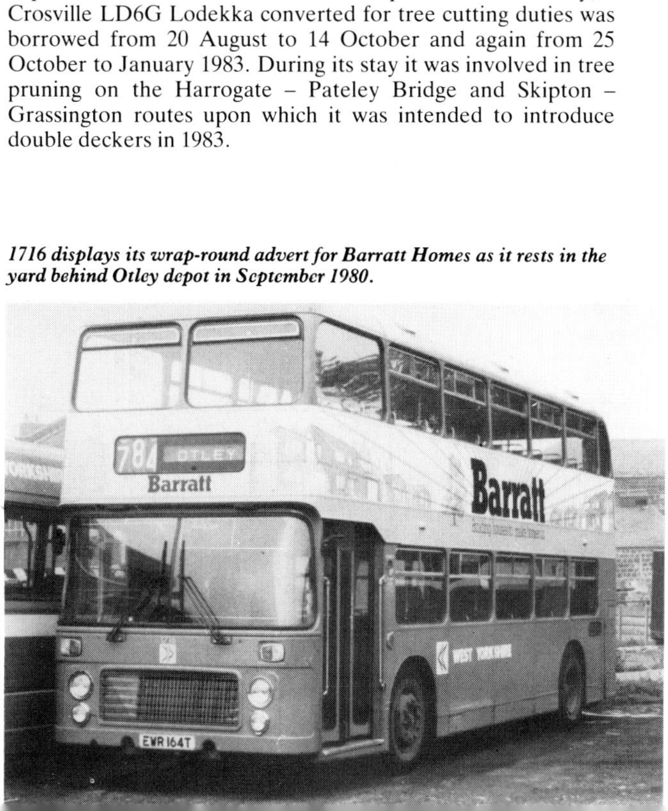

Of the three Duple-bodied Dennis Falcon V coaches operated by West Yorkshire, only 2201 was delivered new to the company. It is seen here arriving in London on a Rapide duty from Bradford.

During May 1982 a start was made on the conversion of the three Leyland VRTs fitted with Leyland engines to Gardner-power. This task was eventually completed in July 1983, thus standardising the large VRT fleet throughout the company. Another programme started during the year was the fitting of Ferodo retarders to the Mk.2 Leyland Nationals, this continuing into the following year.

The first day of 1983 saw the transfer of 5 Bristol VRTs from the main fleet to York and these were followed by a further 4 in May/June. More important however was the entry into service in January of the company's first Leyland Olympian double deckers. Deliveries continued throughout the year and by December no fewer than 31 had taken up their duties. Of these, 10 were fitted with Voith automatic transmission and were from a batch of 15 so equipped for NBC evaluation (the other 5 went to Crosville). The Olympians were not the only new model to make their debut for on 1 January a Duple Special Goldliner 47-seat Dennis Falcon V coach entered service on the London Rapide service. Equipped with video equipment, a toilet and a servery, this was one of a batch of 10 Dennis Falcon Vs purchased by the NBC for evaluation purposes and leased to its operating subsidiaries. More conventional, but of a new type nevertheless were 4 Plaxton Paramount 3500-bodied 50-seat Leyland Tiger coaches and 10 Tigers with Paramount 3200-type 53-seat bodies. Completing the year's new arrivals were a pair of Ford Escort vans and a Transit pick-up for the ancillary fleet.

The new Dennis Falcon proved to be troublesome from the start and during February various coaches had to be borrowed from Trathens and Parks in order to maintain the Rapide service whilst the Dennis was undergoing repair. Even one of Yorkshire Traction's two Dennises of the same type was borrowed on a couple of occasions. After giving more trouble in June a Falcon V was hired from Greenslades of Torquay for two days and it was with no regret that West Yorkshire's example was transferred to United on 11 July. Its replacement eventually arrived at the start of September when a Plaxton Paramount-bodied Leyland Tiger was purchased from Yorkshire Traction. Another secondhand vehicle to be acquired was a Northern General Leyland National which was purchased on 18 January. This however was obtained only for spares and upon its arrival at Harrogate it was immediately dismantled.

Double deck operation on the Yorkshire Dales services from Skipton to Grassington and beyond finally started on 6 February with Grassington depot accommodating double deckers for the first time in its history. This new operation had hardly got underway than rumours began to spread that Skipton depot was to be closed later in the year, thus isolating Grassington from its parent. This took place on 13 August when the doors of Skipton depot were closed for the last time and since that date much dead mileage has been involved in the transfer of buses from Keighley to take up their duties in Skipton. Prior to the closure of the latter's depot, additional fuel storage tanks had to be installed at Grassington and whilst this work was in progress, the company borrowed an AEC Mammoth Major tanker from APT at Lincoln from June until August to provide an additional fuel supply.

Following the introduction by West Yorkshire PTE of pre-paid Saverstrip discount tickets during the summer, West Yorkshire had to equip a large part of their fleet with cancellor machines in which passengers could insert these new travel tickets. These were fitted to a number of dual purpose vehicles as well as stage carriage buses and looked somewhat out of place on a vehicle fitted with coach-type seats. West Yorkshire PTE were

Bristol VRT 1714, complete with Metrobus fleet names carries extensive publicity posters for the P.T.E's 'off peaker' maximum 30p fare as it rests in Keighley bus station in January 1982.

not the only ones to introduce discount tickets however, for on 6 November the company launched a three month experiment in the Harrogate/Knaresborough area under the title of 'Nightrider'. This enabled passengers to purchase a 50p runabout ticket which could be used after 7.00 pm on Monday to Saturday and all day Sunday for use on all the company's services within that area.

Willowbrook-bodied Leopard 2599 looks immaculate in its attractive two-tone blue & white Yorkshire Coastliner livery at York railway station in August 1983.

In order to promote their East Coast services from Leeds, a number of Leopard dual purpose vehicles were repainted into a striking new blue & white livery and lettered 'Yorkshire Coastliner' from May onwards and these soon became a familiar sight on the roads from Leeds to Bridlington and Scarborough via York. The all-over advertising VRT in Morrisons livery was repainted into another predominantly yellow scheme to the order of Lightwater Valley leisure park during the early summer whilst in August, Leyland National 1515 was given all-over advertising for the company's own Montpellier Travel at Harrogate. A further bus to be used for promotional purposes was Olympian 1828 which, although retaining its poppy red & white livery was adorned with some diagonal cream bands and lettering for the Bus & Coach Council campaign exhorting people to travel by bus.

During October, the first of 3 Bristol VRTs to be converted to permanent driver training buses emerged from the company's Harrogate workshops looking striking in its new white livery with red relief. A month later, on 10 November the second such conversion made its debut but this differed from the first by having a detachable front roof dome to enable it to also serve as a tree cutter. Its appearance was ten days too late however, for on 1 November the company had hired one of United's Scarborough sea front service open top Bristol VRTs for tree pruning around Harrogate and Wetherby for a few days.

Finally, on 5 December a new service was inaugurated jointly with West Riding from York to South Milford, a village last served by West Yorkshire in 1934 when they exchanged a former Corcoran route with J. Bullock & Son. Almost a year later, on 29 October 1984, this new service was extended onwards to Pontefract whilst from 3 November to 15 December 1984 a new Saturday only operation was introduced from York to Sheffield under the title of 'Sheffield Shopper'. Earlier in the year, and somewhat surprisingly, York West Yorkshire had started an open top park and ride service in the city, this operating from 23 July to the end of August. Having no vehicles of this type with which to operate this new venture, an open-top Bristol VRT was hired from Southdown for this period as was a similar vehicle

Heading out of the city to Naburn Hospital on route 17A on 5th October 1982, Southdown 511 was one of three Bristol VRTs hired by West Yorkshire from this Brighton-based operator. As well as retaining its operator's fleet names and green livery, its side advertisement still exhorted people to visit Southampton Show. (K. A. Jenkinson)

from Yorkshire Traction. In exchange for the latter, York loaned Traction a conventional VRT – 3739. A further new service to appear during the year was one from Bradford to Lightwater Valley, north of Ripon and this became the domain of the Lightwater all-over advertising liveried Bristol VRT 1748. Taking up the challenge with British Rail, the company entered into a price war on 30 March when they reduced the price of a day

1748 in its predominantly-yellow Lightwater Valley all-over advertising livery at Baildon Bridge on its way from Leeds to Bradford on route 755 in June 1983.

return ticket from Leeds to Harrogate from £2.35 to £1.80 which compared favourably against British Rail's £2.20 return for this same journey. With the opening of part of Otley's new – and long needed – bypass on 4 July, West Yorkshire's services from Ilkley into the town were diverted to use this new road, although outward journeys continued to follow the old route direct along Ilkley Road.

Continuing the company's rationalisation policy, Ilkley depot was closed on 29 September, its 10-strong allocation being divided equally between Keighley and Otley depots. This involved yet more dead mileage, with vehicles now having to run empty from their new depots in order to take up their duties in Ilkley. Over at Harrogate, the row of cottages next to the Central Works unit cleaning shop at Myrtle Road was demolished to provide space for a staff car park.

As far as the fleet itself was concerned, 10 more Leyland Olympians were added, as were 5 Plaxton Paramount-Tigers equipped to Rapide specification, although one of these was painted in a special livery to operate under contract to Ray Denison School Travel of Otley, making numerous sorties to Europe in this capacity. The York fleet gained its first new double deckers since 1981 when it took delivery of 4 Olympians at the start of February. Leyland National 1494 which had spent the first three months of the year at Crosville's engineering workshops at Chester eventually returned home early in April complete with a Gardner engine in place of its original Leyland unit. Although such conversions were by now 'old hat', this was the first undertaken by the company and although it was thought that more might follow, 1494 has remained unique in the fleet. A start was made at this same time on modifications to the B-series long and short Nationals which lacked roof pods. These began to receive a scoop on their roof above the fourth window on the nearside of their body in an attempt to improve the circulation of air within their interiors. A veritable flood of all-over advertising liveries appeared during the year, all involving Bristol VRTs buses of both the main company and York fleets. No fewer than 8 appeared, including 1748 which gained its third consecutive all-over scheme in September. This was somewhat different to the 'norm' however as it re-entered service for a few days in its all-over black base colour (being nicknamed Knightrider by its Bradford depot staff) before being returned to the paint shops to receive its lettering etc. for Radio Aire.

On 28 March, West Yorkshire PTE decided to follow the example set by Tyne & Wear PTE and decreed that all the buses operated by NBC subsidiaries within the county would have to be painted into the corporate PTE livery of Verona Green & Buttermilk, and that this should be undertaken at the earliest possible date. West Riding, Yorkshire W.D. and Yorkshire Traction almost immediately put their repainting programme in hand, but West Yorkshire, not relishing the thought of having to operate a mixed fleet – colour wise – were in no great hurry to follow suit. As far as the company was concerned, only their buses at Leeds, Bradford, Keighley, Otley and Wetherby were to be subjected to the new livery, those at their other depots (which were in North Yorkshire County) retaining their traditional (albeit poppy) red. This obviously would create problems with regard to the inter-depot transfer of vehicles and would in effect split the buses into two separate fleets. Eventually, following pressure from the PTE, a Keighley VRT – 1762 – was taken into central works in early August for its green repaint, but as a result of a dispute over parity pay, the paintshop

The first single decker to succumb to the West Yorkshire PTE livery of verona green and buttermilk was Leyland National 1480, seen here in Bradford in February 1985.

staff refused to complete the bus. It remained in undercoat for over four months before the dispute was resolved and it was not until the end of December that it emerged in its new colours. Even then it was another few weeks before it finally re-entered service. Thereafter, other vehicles were transformed into pseudo-PTE buses – albeit slowly – and as well as VRTs, Leyland Nationals and one or two Olympians gained this new colour scheme.

After rejoicing at getting rid of their Dennis Falcon V coach the previous year, it came as a surprise when, at the start of May this returned from United to re-join the fleet and resume its duties on the Rapide services. Even more surprising was that it was not alone. The two former Yorkshire Traction Falcon Vs which had also been transferred to United came with it, and now West Yorkshire had three of these troublesome machines! As was to be expected, the company soon found themselves unable to cover some Rapide duties as the Falcons languished over the pits in Bradford depot, and after borrowing vehicles from National Travel East with which to maintain the service, they took 2 Rapide-equipped Plaxton-bodied Leopards on hire from Ribble on 16 August, these staying with the company until the end of the year. The 3 Falcons, although officially withdrawn at the end of October continued to put in spasmodic appearances on the Rapide services until the end of December – except for 2202 which was extensively damaged by fire at Bramham Cross Roads on 1 November. The remaining pair never ran again for the NBC, being sold early in 1985 to a dealer. Another noteable withdrawal was that of the company's last remaining Bristol RELL saloon which made its final journeys on 31 October. Happily this has been preserved by a group of staff at the company's Bradford depot, thus ensuring its future. Another hire to take place during the year was that of a United open top Bristol VRT which was borrowed on 7 May (for one day only) in order to take the victorious York City football team on a tour of the city following their promotion to the third division of the football league.

Added to the ancillary fleet during 1984 were a pair of Ford Escort vans whilst the AEC recovery wagon, 4064, was despatched to the local Leyland agents to have its chassis lengthened by about 6ft (between its axles) before returning to receive a new cab etc. A further new Escort van was purchased in 1985, as were a trio of Ford Transits, two of which arrived as chassis/cabs to receive the pick-up bodies removed from the

Specially painted in the former York Corporation livery of dark blue and white to commemorate the 50th anniversary of the Joint Undertaking, 3771 looked extremely smart in its new guise.

To provide cover for the troublesome Dennis Falcon Vs, a pair of Rapide specification Plaxton-Leopards were hired from Ribble from August until December 1984. One of these, 78 loads its London-bound passengers in Bradford Interchange's coach park.

Beginning life in 1973 as a bus, Leyland National 1415 has now been converted into a luxuriously appointed mobile office/hospitality suite and made its debut in its new role in 1986.

vehicles they were replacing. One of the company's oldest Leyland Nationals was taken into the body shop at Harrogate to undergo conversion into a mobile office. This work was only undertaken as and when time allowed, and it was December before it was completed and February 1986 before it undertook its first duty in its new guise.

Carrying NBC's stripey white livery and both West Yorkshire and National names is 2710, a Plaxton Paramount 3200-bodied Leyland Tiger.

Dual-purpose seated Olympian 1857 carries the attractive two-tone blue & white Yorkshire Coastliner livery. The location is the yard behind Bradford depot in September 1985.

York's towing lorry, a Leyland Retriever heads along Station Road, York in 1986 to give assistance to a failed vehicle on the outskirts of the city.

Following this, 2 of York West Yorkshire's Bristol VRTs were taken into the company's central workshops for conversion to open top for use during the summer season at York. On these, work progressed quickly and both were available for service by the start of June.

New arrivals to the fleet comprised 3 more Paramount 3200-Tiger 53-seaters, 3 Tiger-Paramount 3500 48-seaters to Rapide specification, one of which was given a cherished registration number removed from a Lodekka driver training bus, 4 Olympian buses; 10 Olympian dual purpose double deckers and 2 Carlyle-bodied 16-seat Ford Transit minibuses. Of these, the 4 Olympians arrived in PTE Verona green & buttermilk livery, the first – and only – buses delivered new in these colours whilst the 10 dual purpose Olympians sported an attractive blue & white Coastliner livery for use on the East Coast services. The minibuses were finished in a cream colour with brown and red stripes and were lettered Moors-link in preparation for their new duties in the Haworth area, about which more later. York too were included in the year's new deliveries, receiving 4 more Olympians.

A further addition to the fleet during April was a two month-old Rapide-equipped Paramount-bodied Tiger acquired from United. This was required for additional Rapide schedules, and to complete the number of coaches now needed, 3 of the Paramount 3200-bodied Tigers taken into stock the previous year were returned to Plaxton for upgrading to Rapide specification. Later, in October when the Rapide schedules were yet again increased, a Paramount-Tiger was hired from Midland Red West for an extended period. This carried its owner's Euro Cruising livery of silver and green and remained thus painted throughout its stay with West Yorkshire. A less spectacular hire took place in mid-April when a United FLF6G Lodekka driver training bus was borrowed for a short time.

This view of Olympian 1818 taken at Bradford Interchange on de-regulation day, 1986 finds it still wearing its Metrobus green & cream livery and fleet names as it leaves on the 665 service to Skipton.

Apart from the increase in Rapide operations already briefly mentioned, the company's service network witnessed a number of changes, some of which were planned, others which were thrust upon them without prior warning. The first of these happened on 24 February when part of the bridge, over which West Yorkshire services passed, at Kettlewell collapsed. The only alternative route was along roads completely unsuitable to buses and as a result, a local garage owner had to bring passengers down the Dale from Starbotton, Buckden and Hubberton in a Land Rover to meet the bus at Kettlewell on the south side of the bridge. This unforseen curtailment of the company's services in this picturesque part of the Yorkshire Dales continued for some weeks before the offending bridge could be reopened. On 29 April two new services were commenced from Malton to Helmsley, one travelling via Gilling, the other via Nunnington. More wide sweeping were the changes planned for the Haworth/Keighley area in which it was proposed to introduce several new services under the Moors Link banner. These however were fraught with difficulties and never got off the ground until revised plans were implemented more than a year later. Another service applied for was from Bradford to Oakworth via Keighley, Haworth and Mytholmes and this too did not materialise for some considerable time, finally being introduced in February 1986. Still in that general area however, a new service was inaugurated on 25 May from Bradford to Keighley via Queensbury, Denholme and Ponden Mill and a month later from Keighley to Leeming and Keighley to Denholme. All these traversed narrow country roads, and in respect of the infrequent service via Queensbury and Ponden Mill, its operator – Bradford depot – had to borrow a baby National from Keighley as a result of normal length vehicles being unsuitable. Finally, the first buses only traffic lane within the main company area was introduced in Harrogate at the bottom of East Parade on 1 July as a result of road alterations in that area.

Upon the re-introduction of the open-top service in York on 26 May (which required 2 buses), only one of the newly converted York open-top VRTs had been completed and it was thus necessary to hire an open-top VRT from Bristol Omnibus Company until the second York example was ready. This hire was extremely brief and was terminated on 1 June when York were able to provide both buses themselves. Later in June (on the 28th), Leyland National 1412 was stolen from outside Leeds depot and crashed in Stoney Rock Lane whilst being driven by the thief. As a result of its age (it was new in 1973), it was not repaired and was instead withdrawn.

Further all-over adverts appeared on Bristol VRTs and a Leyland Olympian and a memorable occasion occurred on 31 August when the company's last Bristol single deckers – a pair of dual purpose Plaxton-bodied RELHs were withdrawn from service. This marked the end of a long era, with Bristols being the mainstay of the fleet for thirty years. Two more VRTs were converted into permanent driver training buses, although some of the Lodekkas serving in this role still continued to give yeoman service and the company continued to undertake mechanical and body repair work for outside bodies, a practice

Plaxton Paramount 3500-bodied Leyland Tiger coach 2412 carried contract livery for Ray Denison School Travel during 1985 and in connection with this it made regular trips across the channel to Europe.

commenced during the previous year. At Leeds depot several M.O.D. Crash Tenders were overhauled whilst a variety of vehicles received attention at other depots and at the company's central workshops in Harrogate. The two Moorslink-liveried minibuses which had been licenced from 1 August and had spent most of the time tucked away inside Harrogate depot were de-licenced at the end of September, the future of their planned operation still being unknown. Although their re-appearance in December prompted much speculation, their use at Harrogate and Bradford depots was confined mainly to the transportation of staff between the depots and local bus stations, although they did at least earn a little revenue from the occasional private hire job.

The Setright ticket machine era had now almost come to an end and when the last of these were withdrawn from Leeds depot on 1 May, only Keighley depot continued to make the occasional use of this type of equipment. By now the Almex machine had become the company's new standard, this being more sophisticated than its predecessor and able to provide more information for the traffic department.

During 1985 rebuilding work continued at York depot and major alterations began at the company's Keighley premises in June. These were to continue for the remainder of the year in order to update and improve the facilities at both these properties. At Pateley Bridge, planning permission was again sought for the construction of houses on the field at the side of the depot, this having been previously refused two years earlier.

Finally, on 1 November a major managerial restructuring took place when five separate operating districts were created. Each was placed under the control of a District Manager who was supported by a depot engineer and at least one local traffic superintendent. In view of the coming of the new Transport Act, a Tendering and Registration Manager for the continued profitable organisation of the company's service network.

Hired for use on York's new open-top park and ride service in July 1984 was Yorkshire Traction Bristol VRT 924 which is seen here complete with 'York' fleet names.
(K. A. Jenkinson)

The old and the new. Lodekka permanent driver training bus 4066 stands alongside one of its sister Bristol VRTs (in white & red livery) at Harrogate depot in March 1987.

Coaches were placed under the control of a Coaching Manager whilst publicity continued to be handled by a separate department. Following this massive reorganisation, the company made an approach to York City Council with an offer to buy its 50% share in the York West Yorkshire joint undertaking and although this did not meet with a negative response, York Council commissioned an independent agency to assess the four options available. These were : to operate a new joint company; to split the existing operation and form a City of York transport company; to buy out West Yorkshire's share in York West Yorkshire or to sell their share to West Yorkshire. After receiving the agency's report, it was agreed to sell their share to the company and talks were continued in this direction. The negotiations concluded, York West Yorkshire passed into the annals of history on 10 March 1986. On that day, the York fleet was re-numbered into the main company series by the replacement of the '3' prefix to fleet numbers with a '1' and the York fleetname, City crest and NBC 'double N' symbol all disappeared in favour of the new Citibus name introduced for the York-based fleet. As the new fleet name transfers had not arrived at this time, temporary vinyl stickers bearing a mini-version of the new fleet name were applied to all the former YWY buses, these being replaced by the permanent transfers after a few weeks. This then marked the end of joint operating companies within the NBC. The York undertaking had celebrated its Golden Jubilee in 1984 when a VRT had been painted into the old Corporation's colours of dark blue & white, unlike Keighley West Yorkshire which never reached this milestone. A glimpse of what might have been came shortly before the demise of the York undertaking when several of the new Ford Transit minibuses were painted in the old Corporation livery – but as will be seen later, these never entered service in these attractive colours.

Formerly York West Yorkshire 3983 but now renumbered 1983, this VR shows off its new Citibus fleet name as used by the York-based fleet in September 1986.

1985 ended with the introduction of three commuter limited stop services during December, these being from Leeds to Ilkley via Rawdon; from Bradford to Ilkley and from Bradford to Keighley, the latter being a revival of the old X67 which began back in April 1958.

With the new Transport Act beginning to take effect, and with de-regulation looming on the horizon, West Yorkshire, like all other bus operators, had to register all the services they wished to operate commercially after 26 October by the end of February and this took up many hours of management's time in preparatory work. Following the registration of commercially

Temporarily used in all-over yellow livery pending its all-over advertising lettering, 1759 approaches Bradford Interchange on 4 April 1986.

viable services, it was the duty of the PTEs and district councils to assess where additional services were required and to put these out to tender. An entire book could be written on this subject alone, but to suffice in these restricted pages, it can be said that West Yorkshire, through their registrations, intended to continue operations throughout most of their territory following D-day.

Turning for a moment to the fleet, this underwent dramatic change during 1986 with the arrival of a large number of minibuses and double and single deck coaches, but no conventional full-size stage carriage vehicles. Looking first at the coaches, 2 were Duple-bodied Leyland Tigers equipped to a high standard for prestige private hire and tours duties whilst the others were all three-axle double deckers. The first of these to

West Yorkshire's Citibus fleet name and standard legal lettering as applied to Bristol VRT 1985.

arrive were 4 MCW Metroliner 73-seaters equipped to Rapide specification for the London services. Entering service on 1 April these were followed later that month by 4 Plaxton Paramount 4000s – 71-seaters with Neoplan running units, and these too were Rapide coaches for London operations. A further 3 MCW Metroliners took up their duties on 14 May, although these differed from the previous batch by being of the express type with single door and seating for 79 passengers. These had been purchased for use on the Trans-Pennine service from Leeds to Liverpool via Bradford and Manchester which used the M62 motorway for much of its journey. The minibuses began to arrive in quantity from the turn of the year, the first being Carlyle-bodied Ford Transits of which there was to be 36 (plus the 2 already taken into stock in 1985). The 6 arriving in January were all 18-seaters painted in the former York Corporation livery of dark blue & white and were intended for use on the new minibus

The newest coaches to enter the fleet are a pair of Duple-bodied Leyland Tigers which made their debut in 1986. One of these, 2414 was caught by the camera in Edinburgh in September of that year.

2009, one of the MCW Metroliner express vehicles usually to be found on the Trans-Pennine route from Leeds to Liverpool is seen here on a private hire duty in April 1987.

Rapide specification MCW Metroliner 2007 leaves Victoria Coach Station, London in April 1986 at the start of its long journey to Harrogate.

network planned for that city. In the event, the difficulties experienced by the refusal of staff at York to accept this new form of transport resulted in them being placed in store at the closed Ilkley depot, and all received a different livery before their eventual entry into service later in the year. These were followed by a further 29 Carlyle-bodied Transits, some of which were 16-seaters whilst others were 18-seaters and before their entry into service a number of these had their seating increased to carry 20 passengers. Delivered in a plain turquoise-blue livery, these had orange and cream bands added by the company and were emblazened with their 'Hoppa' operating name. The 6 York Corporation-liveried examples were also repainted into this new livery before taking up their revenue-earning duties. Finally, in mid-October a batch of 20 Robin Hood-bodied Iveco Daily 21-seat minibuses arrived – 10 with stage carriage seating, 10 with coach-type seats. All were delivered in the turquoisey blue base coat and had their relief colours and Hoppa names added by West Yorkshire. Before entering service with their owner, a number of the new Transits saw use with other transport undertakings, one being loaned to Southern Vectis on the Isle of Wight from 24 December 1985 until 5 February for use in service, another being used on a new minibus route in Beverley by East Yorkshire Motor Services in May 1986 and 4 being loaned to West Yorkshire PTE during the period August to September/October 1986 for driver training prior to the introduction of their own minibuses. The company's own operation of Hoppas finally commenced on 28 July, not at York where they had been intended earlier in the year but at

Standing in Bradford depot in readiness for its next duty to London is Plaxton 4000 bodied 2003, a 6-wheeler based on a Neoplan underframe and fitted to Rapide specification.

A line up of coaches at Flamingoland in July 1986 shows E.C.W.-bodied 2390 with a rear-end poster for the London service and a variety of applications on the three Plaxton 3500-bodied Tigers 2407, 2409 and 2402.

Carlyle-bodied short wheelbase Ford Transit minibus 101 wearing the MoorLink livery in which it was delivered new poses on Harrogate Stray in August 1985. Its destination blind shows the M3 service to Stanbury via Oldfield, one of the original abortive MoorLink routes. (K. A. Jenkinson)

For a few months during 1986, Plaxton-Leopard dual-purpose 2591 wore a special livery for its duties on the Airport service from Leeds to Leeds/ Bradford airport.

Harrogate on 3 new town services. For this purpose they were equipped with coloured destination blinds and used route letters instead of the more conventional numbers. Specially produced publicity leaflets were distributed during the week before their introduction and it was not long before the little Hoppas became firm favourites with the travelling public. With these small vehicles, the company's services were now able to penetrate housing estates which had previously precluded the use of conventional sized buses and with improved frequencies etc. it was not long before people began to leave their cars at home and make use of public transport. Hoppa operations in Harrogate were increased in September and October with the introduction of more new services and the whole of the town's old local network of routes was revised. Meanwhile, across at York the minibuses – now in standard Hoppa livery of course – finally entered service on 5 October, although they had already become a familiar sight around the city on a variety of other duties before that date. In the Malton area one of York's Hoppas had been used on Saturday duties between Malton and Wintringham during August and on the first day of 1987 an Otley town service was converted to Hoppa operation as was a newly introduced town route in neighbouring Ilkley. At Keighley where it had been intended to use minibuses on the abortive Moors-Link network, 2 Transits finally entered service on 26 October on a mere shadow of what had originally been planned.

As far as conventional buses were concerned, new late night journeys under the PTE's Nightowl banner began on 21 March from Bradford to Baildon and Keighley and these were joined later in the year by certain operations from Leeds to nearby towns. On 25 May all the normal stopping journeys on the 54 service from York to Harrogate were withdrawn on Sundays, being replaced by a new limited stop service between these two towns and three weeks later, on 16 June a new express service supported by West Yorkshire PTE was inaugurated between Leeds and the Leeds/Bradford Airport at Yeadon. Operating hourly for a three-month trial period, a 50p flat single fare was charged for the operaion on this new service, a pair of the company's Plaxton-bodied Leopard dual purpose vehicles were repainted into a special red, black and white livery and were lettered 'Airporter'.

These were not the only vehicles to receive new liveries during 1986 however, for following the announcement under the 1985 Transport Act that all the NBC subsidiaries had to be privatised before 1988, West Yorkshire, along with several other NBC companies decided to break away from the old corporate colour scheme and once again become their own masters. This led to the company's coaching unit adopting a new name and new livery. Using two tone blue and white, Paramount-bodied Tiger 2412 (which had previously sported Ray Denison School Travel contract livery) emerged in March with its new 'Northern Rose' fleetname. Joining it was one of the company's ancillary vehicles, a Transit van, which was also given Northern Rose colours and lettering. More coaches from the private hire fleet received this new image during the year and in each and every instance, these look extremely attractive. Following the transformation of 2412, the stage carriage livery was examined and in April, the company's oldest Leyland National – 1411 – received what can best be described as the old Tilling livery of red and cream, and was completed by the addition of the old traditional style of underlined fleet name as used by the company from 1937 to 1959. Its appearance can only be described as superb and it was not long before a general return to this traditional livery was started. Indeed, all repaints since May 1986 have been into the old Tilling colours and the old – and somewhat incipid – NBC poppy red is now fast disappearing. Following the decision to thus transform the fleet, repainting in the PTE Verona Green & Buttermilk livery ceased in April and priority was given to ridding the fleet of this hue. Fortunately only around 65 buses had ever been placed in these colours and thus the task of eliminating it appeared to be not too difficult. By the end of the year less than 25 of these remained and all had received the company's new livery by June 1987. A further version of the new Tilling red appeared in August when one of the dual purpose-bodied Plaxton Leopards was repainted into a livery of Tilling red below its windows and Tilling cream above, this again being enhanced by the 'new' underlined fleet name.

In order to gain additional revenue, several more Bristol VRTs and Olympians gained all-over advertising liveries during 1986 with some unusually only having this on thier rear panels, and at the end of December no fewer than 22 buses were in complete all-over advertising and 4 in partial advert liveries.

Requiring a heavier recovery lorry able to handle vehicles such as the new double deck coaches etc., the company purchased a DAF-engined six-wheel Leyland Constructor which had previously been used as a demonstrator by its builders. After fitting with recovery booms and other sophisticated towing equipment, this was placed in the care of Bradford depot wearing a new white livery. 2 new-style Ford Transit pick-up trucks were bought for the ancillary fleet as replacements for older vehicles and during September the now almost annual appearance of a United driver training Lodekka was made when an FLF6G was hired for around three weeks. During this same period, one of York's Olympian double deckers suffered severe roof damage

Plaxton-Leopard 2554 is equipped with detachable side and front boards for use when operating the City Tour in York. It is seen here awaiting its passengers outside the railway station in the summer of 1986.

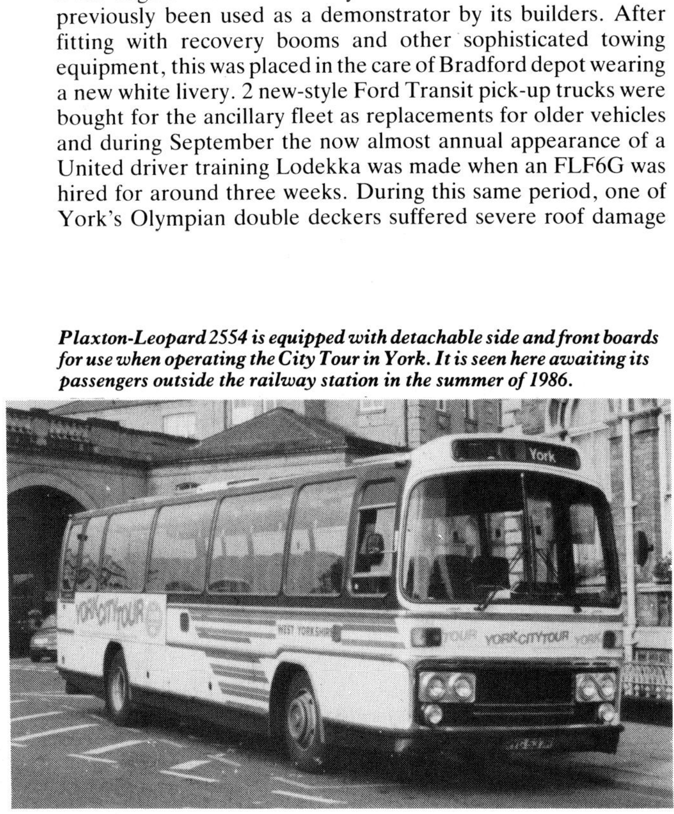

A pair of Robin Hood-bodied Iveco minibuses (141 & 139) stand in Bradford depot immediately after delivery on 12 October 1986. Both wear all-over blue livery and will be sent to the company's bodyshop at Harrogate to have their stripes and Hoppa names etc. applied.

after being driven part way under the low Leeman Road bridge in the city and this was duly returned to ECW for attention. It arrived back at Harrogate in December, its undercoated roof bearing the chalked inscription 'last roof built by ECW, Lowestoft 4.12.86. D. Sword. R.I.P.' obviously reminding one of ECW's pending closure.

The arrival of the minibuses had allowed the withdrawal of a number of Leyland Nationals during the earlier part of the year and, with the forthcoming de-regulation still being something of an uncertainty, rather than dispose of these vehicles it was decided to place them in store. The closed Ilkley depot, which was still owned by the company, was used for this purpose and for a number of months housed several Nationals with their wheels removed and their bright parts coated with grease, alongside new Transit minibuses. The withdrawal of a few was overtaken at the end of October (following de-regulation) by the withdrawal of a large number of Nationals with no fewer than 28 being taken out of service on the 26th of the month. These were followed five days later by a further 6 and by 3 more at the end of December.

Following de-regulation and the demise of West Yorkshire PTE as operators, a start was made on the removal of Metrobus fleet names from all the buses carrying this identity and throughout November standard NBC-type West Yorkshire transfers were applied (yes to Verona green & buttermilk-liveried buses too!). As stocks of these transfers diminished, the Metrobus name was painted out to leave its 'West Yorkshire' portion – in tiny letters – as the only indication as to the vehicle's ownership, other than of course the legal lettering carried, and early in 1987 vinyls bearing a white version of the new underlined fleet name began to be applied.

Coach-seated Robin Hood-bodied Iveco minibus 150 catches the sunshine outside Grove Park depot, Harrogate in May 1987.

A new office was opened in Rougier Street, York on 17 March and following this, the old premises were immediately demolished. Similarly, with the completion of the new mobile office converted from a Leyland National bus, the old Peak trailer office which had served the company so admirably since 1963 was surplus to requirements and was sold in May, its last duties being performed in September of the previous year.

The joint service from York to Pontefract was truncated at Tadcaster on 30 August and in its new shortened form it was taken over completely by West Riding. A couple of months earlier, on 22 June a slight modification had taken place in Keighley with a few of the town services undergoing change. Included in this was the cross-town 706 route which from that date worked on a circular basis on its town centre to Spring Bank section.

By now, privatisation was uppermost in the mind of the company's senior management and plans were already being made for a management bid for the undertaking during 1987, thus completeing the circle from its start 80 years earlier. The bus industry had changed considerably during this long period of time and after having to licence their services through the Traffic Commissioners since 1930, West Yorkshire now found that with de-regulation such procedures were no longer necessary. After a great deal of speculation as to what might happen when full de-regulation occurred on 26 January 1987 after the three months

Still retaining its Metrobus verona green & buttermilk livery but now carrying a 2-line West Yorkshire fleet name was 1764 at Keighley bus station in January 1987.

Although retaining its Metrobus livery of verona green & buttermilk, Leyland National 1491 had lost its corporate fleet name in favour of West Yorkshire titles by January 1987. This had to be placed on the lower side panels rather than in its more usual position on the roof due to the colour of this area and the white of the name transfers.

A temporary expedient to rid vehicles of their Metrobus fleet name in November 1986 involved the painting out of this part of the title to leave the name West Yorkshire in minute lettering together with the P.T.E. slogan as shown in this view of 1971 in Leeds.

'freeze' period, and wondering what new competition might face them, they found that apart from running in fierce competition with Glenn Coaches of Wiggington new York along a route upon which a new service had been started by that independent during 1986 and with Gent Walker Coaches service from York to Dringhouses, their only other challenge came in Harrogate on 26 January 1987 from the newly-formed Harrogate Independent Travel co-operative. Appropriately operating under the name 'Challenger', this new company had been formed by nine former West Yorkshire drivers who between them acquired 6 new NCME-bodied 22-seat Dodge minibuses and opened up a number of new Harrogate town services as well as operating to Knaresborough and Ripon. Although taking this new competition seriously, the company decided not to have a head-on confrontation with the new challenger, but instead to quietly improve their own Hoppa services covering the same area of the town. Before Challenger's challenge was mounted, West Yorkshire had already announced a new 'go-as-you-please' travel ticket for the Harrogate area under the title 'Sparider' which oculd be used on a weekly or a monthly basis and operated on a 2-zone basis. This obviously helped them to stave-off the full effects of new competition, although doubtless a number of passengers must have been lost to Harrogate Independent Travel.

1987 had started less than well when, on 16 January following a dispute, the staff at York depot withdrew their labour. A week later, on 23 January, all the other depots with the exception of Harrogate depot joined in the strike and apart from a tiny handful of drivers at Leeds who gallantly ran the gauntlet and continued to work in order to provide a skeleton service, the company outside Harrogate ground to a standstill. Malton depot decided to return to work on 28 January, but it was not until 5 February that the stoppage finally ended. During the disruption, various independent operators stepped in to maintain some of the company's works and schools contracts as well as covering duties on the York – London and Keighley – London Rapide services.

Since full de-regulation on 26 January, the company has registered a number of variations to its services, most of which have been timetable alterations or minor route changes and undoubtedly more will follow in the light of operating experience. The whole emphasis now is viability as far as operations are concerned and services will continue to be chopped and changed until a fully viable network is achieved. The tendered services too will continue to be regularly examined, and dependant on local authority support, some changes may have to be made in this direction in the future.

The only new competition during the early part of 1987 came in the South Craven area when a local independent, Pinnacle Coaches of Cowling entered the fray on 23 March with a new midibus service from Cowling to Skipton. Although West Yorkshire do not feel seriously threatened by this newcomer, they are quite naturally keeping a watchful eye on the situation and are poised to amend their own services should they feel this necessary.

Whereas a large number of operators throughout Britain have suffered losses of services following de-regulation, which have in turn resulted in slimmer fleets, West Yorkshire have, through careful planning, not only managed to maintain their network but have slightly increased their fleet strength. On 1 January 1986 this totalled 411 passenger vehicles whilst on 1 January 1987 the figure had risen to 421. The main change during the year was of course the large influx of minibuses which have replaced conventional vehicles in Harrogate and York. As new requirements have been mainly for double deck vehicles, it is the single deck fleet that has suffered as the minis arrived and massive inroads have been made into the once large fleet of Leyland Nationals. With an extremely modern fleet, few changes are likely during the next couple of years and no new vehicles are on order for 1987/8, although purchases may be made if demands are created by increased traffic etc. during this period. Meanwhile, following the introduction of the Northern Rose coaching name, this image is being strengthened by the application of this title to all the company's white coaches (including those in National Express livery) in place of the West Yorkshire fleet name, and to the company's travel offices. Additionally, during the early months of 1987 a start was made at eradicating the Citibus fleet name at York and gradually, as vehicles are repainted, this title is being replaced by standard style West Yorkshire transfers. Also disappearing at Keighley and York are the fareboxes, with the buses so equipped being converted to conventional one-person-operation where passengers pay their fare to the driver rather than place it in the farebox and not be able to gain change.

Since the privatisation of National Holidays, the company has still continued to provide coaches under contract in full 'Holidays' livery, but how long this will continue is questionable and it seems likely that West Yorkshire will have to return to pre-NBC days and once again start to provide their own programme of tours and mini-breaks. Similarly, although the provision of vehicles for National Express duties is still maintained (on a 3-year rolling contract), there is no certainty that this will be maintained after the privatisation of National Express, and this too may cause the company to review its position in the long distance service market. Already the company has transferred its Montpellier Travel office at Harrogate and its travel agencies at Keighley and Skipton to National Travelworld and is now

1508, although having received its new Tilling red & cream livery shows no sign of its ownership due to the late delivery of the new-style fleet names. Its fleet number was carried temporarily in the lower corner of its offside windscreen.

Amongst the many former West Yorkshire buses to find further use after withdrawal by the company are two York-fleet Bristol FS6Bs – YDX129 and YDX132 – which are seen here flanking an ex.Lincolnshire Lodekka in the fleet of Kleyn Trucks in Holland. Their new Dutch registration number plates are carried inside their windscreens.

The first bus to receive the company's recently re-introduced smart Tilling red & cream livery was Leyland National 1411. It originally carried its fleet name on its lower side panels, although it later had it repositioned on its roof edge in the now standard position. (K. A. Jenkinson)

1956, one of a pair of flat-windscreened Bristol VRTs converted to open top layout for use in York during the summer months each year. It is seen here during its second season carrying Citibus fleet names.

concentrating all its activities from its other travel offices around its area.

Enroute to Knox on Harrogate Hoppa service T, short wheelbase Ford Transit 125 passes competitor Challenger's Dodge D923DWW outside Harrogate bus station in January 1987. (K. A. Jenkinson)

Bristol VRT driver training bus 4084 also doubles up as the company's tree lopper and as such has been fitted with a detachable front roof dome as can be seen from this view taken at Harrogate depot in July 1987. (K. A. Jenkinson)

A RETURN TO PRIVATE OWNERSHIP

Privatisation was slowly creeping nearer and under the leadership of Giles Fearnley, West Yorkshire's Financial Director, the company's management team had already drawn up plans for the bid they were to submit in an attempt to gain control of the company under the terms of the 1985 Transport Act. It appeared that the management team were however to face strong competition in this direction and it is known that there were several other parties who were also expressing an interest in West Yorkshire's future. Amongst these were Stagecoach of Perth; Carlton PSV Sales; Stuart Johnson and United Transport International. The closing date for bids was Monday 6 April 1987, and as that date passed, much speculation began to circulate as to the successful contender.

The long awaited news finally came in mid-April when National Bus Company took the unusual step of announcing their recommendation of the successful purchaser before the transaction had been completed. The reason for this break in tradition was that the bid being recommended to the Department of Transport was very different to any of the bids that had previously been accepted for other NBC companies. The bid concerned was led by Alan Stephenson who was Managing Director of East Yorkshire Motor Services but included the involvement, on the property side, of Leeds based development company Parkdale Holdings plc. It was because of the involvement of Parkdale that an early announcement was made as it was necessary for them to inform the Stock Exchange of its intentions at the earliest opportunity before it then sought the approval of its shareholders. Mr. Stephenson was no stranger to West Yorkshire having served as Secretary of the company from 1977 to 1985. His involvement with East Yorkshire which was already privatised gave rise, however, to questions regarding potential conflict of interest between that company and West Yorkshire because they shared common boundaries in part of North Yorkshire. National Bus Company, however, stated that in their view there would be no such conflict of interest although this seemed strange in view of the fact that West Yorkshire PTA had been refused the opportunity to bid for the company on the grounds that such a move would be anti-competitive.

While the Parkdale bid was being considered, West Yorkshire continued its business of operating buses and coaches without any noticable change. A number of new summer services commenced on 17 April, most of which were to operate on Sundays and at Bank Holidays and operated into the heart of the picturesque Yorkshire Dales and in addition a new York city tour was inaugurated which was to run at Bank Holidays and then daily from 23 May to 27 September at frequent intervals using the

2705, a Plaxton Paramount-bodied Leyland Tiger coach had gained Northern Rose fleet names by the time this view was taken inside Bradford depot on 2 May 1987. (K. A. Jenkinson)

Moving towards privatisation, poppy red-liveried Leyland Olympian 1806 climbs towards Denholme in June 1987. Gone are its Metrobus fleet names and NBC symbols and in their place is its owner's name in two line styling. (K. A. Jenkinson)

Withdrawn Leyland National 1422 languishes in the yard of Bradford depot. Still wearing its NBC poppy red livery it retains its Metrobus fleet name on its roof edge whilst at the rear displays its owners name and NBC symbol. (K. A. Jenkinson)

Still in poppy red livery in August 1987, Bristol VRT 1746 seen here on the forecourt of Otley depot has gained white traditional style fleet names in place of the Metrobus title previously carried. (K. A. Jenkinson)

open top Bristol VRTs. The 'original' guided York City Tour was reinstated for the Summer on 12 April and, as in previous years operated each day except Saturday through to 2 November. Exploiting the new Transport Act's de-regulation effects to the full, minor service changes were now being undertaken almost on a weekly basis with journeys being added, withdrawn or modified to take into account passenger's needs and a watchful eye was also being trained on areas which had not previously enjoyed regular forms of public transport. Following the introduction of a further Hoppa service in Harrogate on 30 March which served the Chatsworth Grove and Coppice Way areas of the town, it was decided to introduce hail and ride facilities to Harrogate's Hoppa network, this taking effect from 8 June. Meanwhile, a month earlier a number of additional services were introduced on weekends and at Bank Holidays to serve the North Yorkshire Moors and towards the end of May the company launched its Castle Howard Hoppa service with minibuses providing two journeys in each direction from York to Castle Howard (of Brideshead Revisited fame) each Tuesday, Thursday and Saturday and at Bank Holidays. At the other side of the company's territory a new Hoppa service was started in Keighley on 1 June, running hourly between the bus station and Tarn Hill and serving the Shann Park residential area. Still in Keighley, as a result of public demand, the service from the bus station to Airedale Hospital which had been discontinued on 26 October 1986 was reinstated as from 29 June, running half hourly each day except Sundays when two journeys were provided to coincide with hospital visiting times.

Last, but by no means least, was the fresh batch of tenders issued on 28 May by the local authority in West Yorkshire. A formidable list, this included no fewer than 20 West Yorkshire routes which had been operated with local authority support since de-regulation and with the closing date not being until 30 June, it could only be speculated which – if not all – the company would ultimately retain.

On the competitive front, West Yorkshire had fared better than most, and other than the independents previously mentioned, the only new areas of competition were again in York where Paul Cowell introduced a rival Poppleton – York service and where Reynard Pullman gained the tender for the Technical College to Memorial Gardens Park and Ride service.

The fleet, as predicted in the previous chapter, underwent few changes during the early part of 1987 other than for the mass

Still sporting its NBC poppy red & white local coach livery, Plaxton-Leopard 2590 has had its NBC-style fleet name replaced with a white version of West Yorkshire's new standard logo. (K. A. Jenkinson)

Bristol VRT 1981 in immaculate Tilling red livery precedes poppy red-liveried 1726 with rear end advertising across Haworth bridge early in July 1987. (K. A. Jenkinson)

A pair of withdrawn Leyland Nationals in store at the rear of Bradford depot show 1455 in NBC poppy red livery and 1468 still adorned in Metrobus verona green & cream. (K. A. Jenkinson)

Coach-seated Robin Hood Iveco Fiat Hoppa 156 shows its rear advertisement as it rests outside Grove Park depot, Harrogate with sister vehicles in July 1987. (K. A. Jenkinson)

withdrawal of Leyland National single deckers, some of which were later reinstated before again being taken out of service. A reserve fleet had by now been created in order to provide engineering support wherever and whenever this was needed and this comprised 14 Leyland Nationals, 4 Leyland Leopard coaches and the 2 open top Bristol VRTs. In a somewhat complicated fashion, these 20 vehicles were further subdivided into replacement, traffic and engineering sub-categories and not all the vehicles contained therein were licenced for immediate use. Together with the 35 vehicles held for disposal as at 1 May, these were causing the company some embarrassment in terms of storage space and earlier in the year it had been found necessary to install 14 of the withdrawn Leyland Nationals and a withdrawn Leopard dual purpose vehicle in the old depot at Ilkley which, despite having been closed in 1984 had still not been sold.

The larger Ford Transit Hoppas were all converted from 18 to 20seaters by the removal of their luggage pens in an attempt to increase their revenue-earning capacity, only to be converted back to 18 seaters during the late summer as a result of complaints by passengers regarding the lack of luggage space. Having operated in an unblemished livery since their introduction, the minibuses began to gain conventional-type rear adverts during April and, as was perhaps to be expected, some months later the first appeared in all-over advertising livery.

The head office at West Yorkshire in East Parade, Harrogate has changed little over the years as far as its external appearance is concerned as this late 'seventies view shows. (K. A. Jenkinson)

Plaxton dual purpose-bodied Leopard 2559 shows off its new Tilling red & cream livery in Keighley bus station as it works a stage carriage duty on the 701 service in July 1987. (K. A. Jenkinson)

Bristol VRT 1755 in all-over advertising livery for National Travelworld approaches Bradford Interchange on a 665 journey from Haworth early in 1987. (K. A. Jenkinson)

Prior to this however, a new form of part-overall advertising began to gain popularity throughout Britain in which only the rear of buses were so painted, the sides and front being retained in normal fleet colours. Following this new trend, West Yorkshire secured contracts for several such advertisements which were not confined to their double deck vehicles, but also featured on some of their Hoppa minibuses.

By the middle of the year, repainting into the smart Tilling red & cream colour scheme was progressing at a rapid, with the emphasis – as stated earlier – being on ridding the fleet of its Metro-green and cream-liveried buses as quickly as possible. This was achieved during June when Leyland National 1002 and Bristol VRT 1990 were outshopped in red and VRT 1760, the last green & cream bus was delicenced for overhaul. Indeed, by the end of June the old NBC poppy red was in the minority with the repainting into the brighter, traditional livery having passed the half-way stage.

As a result of increased double deck vehicle requirements, the company surprisingly purchased 4 secondhand Bristol VRTs from Alder Valley South early in May and these arrived at Harrogate between 5 and 9 of that month. Two of these new acquisitions had already had a string of previous owners, having been new in 1973 to Maidstone & District and later serving with Hastings & District before joining Alder Valley. Both differed from West Yorkshire's own VRT's in being of 13ft.5in. height instead of 13ft.8in. and as a result, when painted in their new owner's Tilling red livery, the cream centre band could not be continued across the front above the windscreens. They further differed from West Yorkshire's VRTs by having seating for 77 passengers instead of the more customary 74. Of the remaining pair, one was a standard 13ft.8in. high 70 seater dating from 1972

Recently acquired low height Bristol VRT 1700 which began life with Alder Valley is seen here before entering service with its new owner. Retaining its coach-type seating, it has been painted into the attractive two-tone blue & white Yorkshire Coastliner livery. (K. A. Jenkinson)

New to Maidstone & District and later serving with Hastings & District and Alder Valley South, low height Bristol VRT 1949 joined West Yorkshire in May 1987. Seen here at Harrogate depot a few days before entering service with its new owner, it can be seen that as a result of its low height the cream centre band cannot be continued across the front above the windscreen. (K. A. Jenkinson)

110, one of Harrogate depot's long wheelbase Carlyle-bodied Ford Transit minibuses was repainted into a predominantly all-over advertising livery in July 1987. It is seen here on 4 August picking up its passengers outside Harrogate bus station. (K. A. Jenkinson)

Posed for the photographer outside Grove Park depot, Harrogate in August 1987 is Northern Rose-liveried Plaxton-Tiger 2412 and NBC poppy red Olympian 1810.

(numbered 1947 by its new owners) whilst the other was a 13ft.5in. high example of 1975 vintage which was fitted with 70 coach-type seats. Rather than refit it with normal bus seats, it was decided to keep it as it was and to repaint it into the blue & white Yorkshire Coastliner livery. All four of these acquired vehicles were eventually placed in service on 1 July from Keighley depot, although having been retrospectively fitted with power steering which raised the height of the steering wheel by several inches, they soon proved unpopular with staff.

Some nine days later, an unfortunate accident on the fringe of Otley claimed two of the company's vehicles when National Express-liveried Leopard 2588 collided almost head on with Olympian 1863, causing extensive damage to both vehicles. This sad episode was followed some few days later by the destruction of a newly repainted all-over advertising Ford Transit Hoppa which was hit broadside by a car whilst in service in Harrogate. Although all-over advertising was far from dead as far as West Yorkshire was concerned, the trend sweeping the country of rear-end advertising was already making a large impact on the company's fleet with several Bristol VRTs, Leyland Olympians and Hoppa minibuses receiving advertising in this new style in a wide variety of bright colours. Finally, it is worthy of mention that two of the remaining Bristol FS6B Lodekka driver training vehicles have recently been overhauled for continued use and, that unlike their VRT sisters, they have not been repainted in a predominantly white livery but in full Tilling red & cream – a nice reminder of the fleet in its earlier days.

Freshly repainted Tilling red Bristol VRT 1743 is unique in the fleet in having a West Yorkshire fleet name below its windscreens. (K. A. Jenkinson)

Meanwhile, on 23 July 1987 it was announced that following approval by the Secretary of State for Transport, Mr. Alan Stephenson and the company senior management were to buy the entire share capital of West Yorkshire. As a consequence, Parkdale Holdings plc were acquiring the properties presently vested in the company, but in giving its approval to the deal, National Bus Company had satisfied itself that West Yorkshire would have the ongoing use of all those properties that it needed for the running of its business. West Yorkshire will, therefore, have leases of the majority of those properties that it had previously owned.

Completion of the sale took place on 25 August following the formal approval to the property side of the deal having been given by Parkdale's shareholders at an extraordinary general meeting held on 19 August 1987.

Prior to this final development taking place, Mr. Giles Fearnley replaced Mr. Brian Horner as Managing Director of West Yorkshire on 1 August, Mr. Horner having made his intentions to leave the company known several months earlier, and we wish both gentlemen well in their new roles.

What then of the future? Returning to the private sector, West Yorkshire Road Car Co. Ltd. will undoubtedly continue to grow from strength to strength and its solid position within the area which it has served for more than 80 years will ensure that the company has a long and healthy future. Despite the recent changes brought about by the 1985 Transport Act, West Yorkshire have already proved that they can successfully meet new competition and will no doubt continue to do so in the years ahead.